The collaboration for this book came from two diverse sources with one common objective -- to create a foundation encyclopedia for an ancient but little known art form, the hand crafted cameo.

Ed Aswad, Commercial/Industrial Photographer and owner of a large cameo collection, and Michael Weinstein, a Jewelry Dealer with an impressive accumulation of antique jewelry, became acquainted during a "Show and Seek" situation. When Ed (seeking to add to his inventory) asked Michael (hoping to exchange some of his) about the availability of shell cameos, their dialogue uncovered a mutual interest in these unique shell carvings.

Over time, the further the pair discussed the market and background of the cameo, the more apparent became the fact that there wasn't enough information "out there" to satisfy their combined curiosities. Research uncovered one book, *Cameos*, by Cyril Davenport, published in 1900, but concentrating on stone cameos. That there were few other written documents about cameos in general, or shell cameos specifically, was indeed a disappointment to them.

More communications and more frustrations made it imperative the pair enter into a liaison to co-author a book expanding on cameo knowledge, styles and prices. Encouraged by Dan Alexander of Books Americana, the two utilized their individual talents; Aswad to photograph some of his (and others) cameos, and Weinstein to compile, analyze and produce the text.

This book then, marks a major step toward a greater enlightenment, understanding, and enjoyment of these centuries old treasures.

Descending down through families, through collections in museums, even tucked away in antique stores, the cameo excites and inspires the viewer to enjoy the object for its craftsmanship alone. Probing the meaning of scenic or mythological detail they portray, adds still another dimension to fascinate the most serious collector or casual viewer. It is for the novice and the expert that this book is published.

Inquiries into the specifications and descriptions in this book, or questions on the gems photographed, are warmly invited. The authors hope to make available more material as time and demands warrant. Correspondence should be directed to:

Carriage House Photography
496 Chenango Street
Binghamton, NY 13901
This is the same address for: Cameo Collectors Society

Ed Aswad
Photographer/Collector

Michael Weinstein
Collector/Co-Author

$12⁹⁵

The Art and Mystique of

Shell Cameos

Identification and Value Guide

by
Ed Aswad
and Michael Weinstein

BOOKS AMERICANA INC

ISBN O-89689-079-1

i

TABLE OF CONTENTS

IDEAL SHELL STRUCTURE FOR CAMEOS

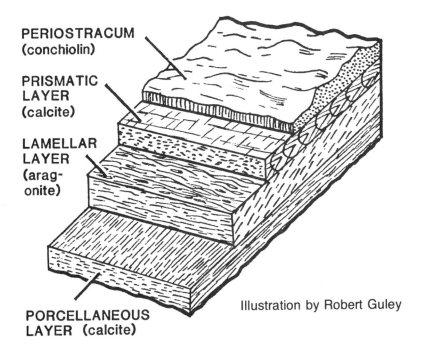

PERIOSTRACUM
(conchiolin)

PRISMATIC
LAYER
(calcite)

LAMELLAR
LAYER
(arag-
onite)

PORCELLANEOUS
LAYER (calcite)

Illustration by Robert Guley

COMMON SHAPES OF CAMEOS

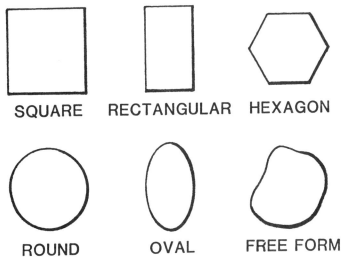

SQUARE   RECTANGULAR   HEXAGON

ROUND   OVAL   FREE FORM

CAMEO DEFINITIONS

There is much confusion when it comes to defining the word "cameo". Not only are the origins of the word unclear, but there is little agreement on what constitutes a "genuine" cameo. Even respected references such as World Book Encyclopedia contain contradictory information:

"...artificial cameos are made from various kinds of shells..."

Since when are shells "artificial"?

In order to arrive at a clear, concise explanation of what a cameo is, it is necessary to examine word origins as well as current definitions.

Some historians believed the word "cameo" to have derived from the Hebrew/Arabic word "kamea", meaning a charm or amulet. This theory is disputed by language experts who maintain that it is only by phonetic coincidence that the two words are related. The root meaning of "kamea" -- to fasten or tie -- is unrelated to the Latin root of the Italian word "cameo" (or "cammeo") which means "to engrave". It is, perhaps, not by accident nor by coincidence that the two words were thought to be related. Mystic lore regarded cameos as having great power as medicinal amulets, enabling the wearer to ward off disease and death. Whether this was due to the material the cameo was carved from, or to the subject matter depicted, or to a combination of both, is not clear. The latter possibility, however, would endow the amulet with the greatest potency.

Another link between the words "kamea" and "cameo" may have been established with the legend of the ancient Israelites -- the Biblical "Children of Israel" -- engaging themselves in cameo "handiwork" during their forty year sojourn in the "wilderness" following the Exodus from Egypt. Other than this "circumstantial" evidence there is no clear connection between the two words.

Two other Hebrew words possibly related to cameo are "kimo" which means "like" as in "likeness" and "kam" (or "kama") meaning "rise" or "risen". Since cameos exhibit a "likeness" and surfaces that are "risen" it is not illogical to hypothesize that the root word(s) to "cameo" might be derived from these two Hebrew words.

Other Arabic words that have been associated with cameo are: "kamkhat" which means encrustation or coating; "kamaut" which translates as "the camel's hump"; and "camant" meaning flower.

It's easy to understand the relationship of the first two of these three Arabic words to "cameo". At first glance, a cameo may appear to have a layer or "coating" of material that projects from the surface like a "camel's hump". Perhaps the third word, "camant" is a metaphor for beauty, signifying the inherent beauty of a cameo; or perhaps flowers were commonly depicted on cameos of the time.

The latter explanation is supported by the fact that many Moslems might consider the depiction of a woman as immodest and a violation of the Koran. Therefore, cameos carved by Arabs would more likely depict non-human objects of beauty, such as flowers.

The ancient word most directly connected to cameo is the Latin "cammaeus", generally translated as "engraved gem". The two major styles of engraving are: "intaglio" where the carving or sculpting is done below, or into, the surface of the stone; and "relief" where the design projects outwards from the stone's background.

Although many antique dealers and jewelers continue to refer to intaglio gems as cameos, it is apparent that the earliest use of "cameo" referred to gems that were carved in relief.

It is useful for both the collector and the jeweler to be aware of the three types of relief and the difference between a "sculpture" and a "relief". In art, a sculpture is defined as a figure that stands alone in three full dimensions. Thus, it can be viewed, and appreciated, from any vantage point. A relief, however, can be viewed and appreciated from most, but not all vantage points since it is only a "partial sculpture" in that the third dimension, the depth or thickness, is partially complete because it is attached to, and rises from, a flat background. In a high relief the depth of the designs is more than half (of the implied depth). Very few cameos exhibit high relief, the most notable exceptions being lava and ivory ones. Many cameos exhibit half relief (semi-relief) but the most common cameos are done in low relief (bas-relief), where the actual depth of the design is less than half of the implied depth (as opposed to the perceived depth which can, on a well carved cameo, appear to be much more than half of the implied depth).

On close examination, many low relief carvings will appear to be nearly flat, as are the designs on most coins. This will not necessarily detract from the appeal of the carving.

A new dimension of artistic skill and esthetic appeal was added to cameo carving when it was discovered that many stones -- and later, shells -- were made of different colored layers or bands. This allowed the artist to create a striking contrast between the raised (relief) layer and the flat (background) layer. This discovery, inevitably led to a narrowing of the definition of "cameo".

"A carving in relief utilizing the layering characteristics of the material to achieve a color contrast between the raised design and the background."

A purist would narrow this definition even more by restricting the "material" a cameo is made from to naturally occurring substances only.

IDENTIFYING CAMEOS: IMITATION OR REAL?

Webster's Dictionary defines imitation as a copy, likeness, resemblance, or a counterfeit. According to this definition, collectors of the Renaissance era were correct in labeling shell cameos as imitations. Shells had just been discovered to be an ideal, natural, medium for cameo carving. The different colored, cross-sectional layering in certain shells resembled that of stones traditionally utilized by cameo carvers for centuries. The new carvers of shells even copied the scenes found on older stone cameos.

It was not long, however, before shell cameos were accepted as genuine. They fit the narrow criteria by which most collectors and artists defined a genuine or "real" cameo:

"A carving in relief done on a naturally occurring

substance which contains different colored layers. The carving must incorporate the contrasting layers in different aspects of the design; most commonly by differentiating between the background and the foreground. The carvings must be done by hand."

By this definition, the only "real" cameos are those carved from appropriate stones, shells, and possibly, wood. A cameo is a particular subcategory of engraved gems. So-called "cameos" carved from materials such as lava, ivory, glass, opal, and even eggshells, marble, bone, nuts, and rubber have, through the centuries been mistakenly identified as "real". So too, have relief carvings executed in every precious and semi-precious gemstone known to mankind, including diamonds. By applying this exact, unambiguous, definition to the identification of genuine cameos, the task of indentification becomes easier. This does not diminish the attractiveness, the importance, or the artistic value of engraved gems -- or even some imitations -- that do not completely fit the definition.

For example so-called cameos made from glass or composite paste were often of exceptional artistic quality. Even in ancient Rome, these imitations were popular and sought after by those who could not afford the more expensive stone carvings. Today, many of these imitations are knowingly included in the finest collections of ancient artifacts.

The ancient manufacturers of "vitreous" pastes, as they are known in the lapidary trade, became so expert that they were able to produce material with different layers of color. Many artists turned to this material because it was easier to carve than stone. Its relative softness enabled them to impart greater detail into their creations. In addition, they could now mass produce a quality work by utilizing the initial carving to make a mold from which additional, nearly identical looking cameos could be produced.

Many artists preferred artificial materials because of the hidden flaws that could be encountered in natural ones. These could include natural cracks, holes, and impurities. Even non-uniform banding was considered undesirable, although the most accomplished artists incorporated this feature into their final design. One of the worst flaws, from an artistic standpoint, was that of "doubling" when the layers parted from one another. These problems were avoided with the use of artificial and composite materials.

To collectors, the most exasperating type of imitation cameo is made from natural materials. The relief portion of a carving made from one material is glued to a flat background material -- usually of the same material, but of a different color -- to create a nearly perfect, counterfeit cameo. These imitations are difficult to detect. Only through careful study, usually with a magnifying lens, can they be identified.

During the 20th century, the most common material from which imitation cameos were made was plastic. This should not be surprising since plastic is cheap, colorful, and easy to mold. Most imitations in plastic are easily detected. Not only do they look and feel like plastic, but they are much lighter in weight than an equivalent stone cameo would be. Compared to an equivalent shell cameo the plastic imitation lacks the irregular lines and "facets" that are the telltale result of hand carving. (See page 152)

When held up to the light a shell cameo is translucent, the relief portion being visible as a silhouette. (See page 46) Most plastic cameos show little, if any, translucency. Shell cameos are usually relatively thin, with the curve of the shell apparent on the reverse. Imitations are typically flat on the reverse and relatively thick in relation to the relief. They also fail the "acid" test. There is usually no visible reaction when a drop of nitric is placed or composite material, whereas a natural, organic substance such as shell will "bubble". Remember to handle the acid with care; test the reverse of the cameo, if possible (the acid may cause discoloration or leave a stain); wipe off the acid as quickly as possible; and ask permission before performing this test on other's possessions. It is better to have an experienced jeweler or precious metals dealer perform this test; they might, in fact, be able to identify or authenticate the "cameo" in queston before performing the acid test.

One way to differentiate between genuine stone and imitations is by the "lip test". When a genuine stone is

4

placed against one's lip it should feel noticeably colder than an imitation. This test works better if the material being tested has been out in the open for a few minutes, away from direct light.

The best way to identify genuine cameos and to protect yourself from acquiring fakes is to deal with a knowledgeable and reputable dealer who will guarantee the authenticity of your purchase, Make sure you understand the dealer's definition of a cameo and what it is, specifically, that you are purchasing. All the while, you should be gaining knowledge to help protect yourself from "honest" mistakes and ignorance, as well. The effort and vigilance will be worth it!

WHERE CAMEOS ARE MADE

The art of cameo carving, a distinct form of gem engraving, is thought to have originated in ancient Greece and ancient Rome. Through the ages, the centers of cameo cutting remained in Italy. During the Renaissance, however, that spotlight was shared by artists in France and, to a lesser degree, England. Even the United States shared the distinction for a brief period during the Art Nouveau years of the early 1900's. *Scientific American,* in 1916, reported that as many as 60 craftsmen, in the New York area alone, were individually engaged in the design and production of cameos.

Even today there are individual cameo production carvers in places outside of Italy including the well known Ute Klein Bernhardt of Oak Park, Illinois. Though she is more strictly known for gem engraving, she sometimes uses multicolored or banded stones to carve "true" cameos.

Stone cameos are also being cut in Germany, by laser and ultrasonic beams. The end product exhibits artistic balance and stunning detail and is manufactured from natural, layered stone. Purists, however, might not recognize these as genuine cameos because they were not cut directly by hand.

The majority of today's cameo artists still reside in Italy and are concentrated, mostly, in the small city of Torre del Greco. With a population of over 100,000 people, this city is situated at the foot of the legendary volcano, Vesuvius, overlooking the Bay of Naples.

Torre del Greco has been described as a:

"typical little Southern Italian city, with beauty and squalor side by side. At noon the market square is crowded with gesticulating salesman, swarms of ragged children, and bustling house wives. In the evening the sidewalk cafes resound with political argument. The most important news is, of course, 'Cameos are coming back.' "

This sentiment must have echoed through the ages as there is archaeological evidence for cameo cutting in the area dating back to Roman times.

It seems almost natural that Italy, in general, and Torre del Greco, in particular, became a center for cameo cutting.

There is easy access to three great natural resources utilized for cameo carving: lava, coral, and conch shells. Cameos made from these materials became very popular following the 15th century. That, along with the relative ease and reduced expense of cutting these softer "stones" -- as well as the reduced expense of acquiring them -- enabled, sometimes, hundreds of cutters to thrive in this area. And when, during the Victorian Era, the popularity of the shell cameo eclipsed that of all others combined, the artisans of Torre del Greco turned their talents, almost exclusively, to producing cameos in shell. Today, the majority of cameos produced in this city come from five "factories". One can still stroll down old, narrow cobblestone streets, however, and hear the echo of cameo carvers fashioning their miniature creations at a workbench in the home.

TREASURE HUNTING: WHERE TO FIND CAMEOS

It is said that the "true" collector gets as much joy out of the hunt as he or she gets from the final "catch". Not all people, however, are collectors looking forward to the vagaries of the hunt. Therefore, it might be sufficient to check out local jewelry stores to find a cameo suitable to one's taste.

While most jewelry stores carry a small selection of cameos, it is likely that only those with estate collections have examples of old and unusual ones. Even the largest of such establishments, including most antique jewelry stores, is unlikely to possess more than a handful of fine, old cameos. The reason for this, plain and simply, is a basic law of economics. As time passes, the supply of old cameos is diminished by the ever-increasing demand for them.

Fortunately, some of the supply ends up in museums. Almost every large museum owns a representation of fine cameos with classical motifs, usually carved in stone. Many private and small public museums also boast examples of cameo jewelry.

Though a museum experience may be culturally and artistically satisfying, it does not satisfy the desire to own a piece of art. In addition, cameo owners seem to enjoy gazing at and caressing their minature art carvings.

There are other places that one can hunt for cameos successfully, including antique stores, antique shows, flea markets, house and garage sales, auctions and even grandma's jewelry box -- not without her permission, of course -- but the best places to find a variety and concentration of cameos are: 1) Large antique shows, particularly, antique jewelry shows -- listings for which can be found in antique magazines and newspapers; 2) Downtown jewelry "districts" found in most large cities such as New York City's 47th street "diamond district" and Boston's "Jeweler's Building"; and 3) Torre del Greco, Italy, the world center for cameo manufacturing (see chapter on "Where Cameos Are Made").

Perhaps in the future, we can look forward to a jewelry show whose main feature is cameos.

BLACK CAMEOS

In ancient Rome, cameos depicting Negroids (Black Africans) were highly prized and sought after. Since the figures that were represented on cameos of this era were usually subjects of veneration, it is likely that the Black African was one, too. That these ancient Romans were so fascinated with the regal, chiseled features of some Blacks is no surprise. Like the Greeks before them, Romans of "high culture" had an almost mystical preoccupation with characteristics of the human body.

Not until the early Renaissance, in the 15th century, was there a revival of this general trend, accompanied by renewed interest in "Black" cameos. Though the Renaissance persisted, however, the interest in "Black" cameos did not. Consequently, examples of this style cameo are extremely rare and found only in stone. Do not mistake cameos with light background and dark relief for a "Black" cameo. Though these "reverse" cameos are also rare, a true "Black" cameo figure must exhibit "African" features.

In 1850 an Englishman created the famous Cameo Habille. It is an exquisite carving of a Black African woman adorned with diamond-studded earrings and hair ornaments (today, "cameo habille" refers to any cameo-figure adornments set with stones).

Up until recently, this was the last known (publicly) "Black" cameo. In 1990 a New York City photographer, turned jewelry designer, Coreen Simpson, created a cameo she calls "The Black Cameo" for "today's African-American woman". In keeping with this contemporary theme, the designer chose a profile that "reflected the physical diversity of black women." (See photo on page 154)

The resulting "cameo" is made from slate fused to a lucite background which is mounted onto a brooch of silver or gold-tone white metal. They are available at several boutiques in the New York area and can be ordered through the Cameo Collectors Society (Box 455 Southview Station, Binghamton, N.Y. 13903-0455).

9

CAMEO FRAMES AND MOUNTINGS

Cameos were not just framed for use in jewelry. They are also found as decorative ornaments on some pieces of furniture, tableware, and jewelry boxes. Some cameos carved from a complete, whole shell were utilized for lamp shades. This is a wonderful way to backlight a cameo, creating a pleasing, three dimensional effect (see illustration F-23 on page 46). Other cameos, prized for their artistic beauty, were framed to be hung on a wall or placed on a mantlepiece.

Through the ages, however, most cameos were mounted to be utilized as jewelry. Examples can still be found of almost every type, including rings, earrings, pins, pendants, brooches, bracelets, lockets, cufflinks, watchfobs, belt buckles, and sweater clips.

Frames, like the cameos themselves, come in all shapes and sizes, the most popular being the oval. Although many cameos are mounted, and held in place, with prongs, most are "bezel set". A bezel is a metal ribbon -- sometimes referred to as a "gallery wire" -- that is wrapped around the perimeter and folded over the edge of the cameo. It is usually surrounded by the more decorative part of the frame, although the bezel itself can be decorative. One recent jewelry supply catalog illustrated more than a dozen different styles of gallery wire.

Although usually machine made today, cameo frames manufactured prior to the 20th century were fashioned at least in part, by hand. Even today, shell cameos must still be set by hand since no two can be exactly alike in their curvature, thickness, and contours.

See photo section "Parts of Cameo Frames" beginning on page 169.

CARING FOR CAMEOS

As a unique combination of jewelry and art, cameos should be cared for properly. There are two basic concerns: storage and cleaning. To prevent damage and corrosion to the frame, cameo jewelry should be stored in a secure, clean and dry place. Even gold frames become tarnished due to pollution and oxidation of the alloys in the metal. Careful storage can retard this natural process as well as prevent stones and shells from becoming chipped. It is mistakenly believed that the hard stones many cameos are carved from are nearly indestructible. This is untrue. Even the hardest stones, including diamonds, are brittle and can be chipped by another hard object.

Unlike shells -- and "soft" stones such as pearl, opal, turquoise, and lapis -- hard stones do not require any special, additional care. Hard stones are prized, in part, because they are virtually immune to aging and the elements.

Shells and "soft" stones, however, are subject to discoloration and cracking from dryness, aging, and the elements. They require more vigilance and care, whether they are being used or stored. This perceived vulnerability likely contributes to the great emotion some owners feel towards this category of jewelry.

Fortunately, caring for them is simple. Because these materials are porous -- compared to hard stones -- they require periodic "moisturizing". This is done, preferably, with a fine oil such as mineral or baby oil, or oil of wint-o-green."* The latter is recommended by "old-timers" and is available at drugstores. (It also has the benefit of leaving the cameos with a pleasant, fresh odor. The oil can be applied with a finger, a Q-tip, or a cloth. It should be allowed to "soak in" for a few hours or overnight. Then, the excess or residue should be wiped off. This process should be performed once or twice a year, especially after cleaning.

Cleaning cameos is also simple as long as one is wary of dislodging small stones that might be set in the frame

*Some jewelers even prefer natural body oil, such as that obtained from the face or forehead.

or in the cameo itself. A gentle scrubbing with a soft bristle toothbrush in a mild soap and water solution is the most popular method. Some people prefer a mild solution of ammonia and water (similar to window cleaners) or a jewelry cleaner (also similar to many window cleaners, but much more expensive). Whatever solution used should be rinsed off immediately and thoroughly with warm water. Never soak shell cameos or "soft" stones in any cleaning solution for more than 30 seconds. This will avoid any visible erosion that can be caused by most solutions.

Like any investment in jewelry and art, cameos are worth caring for!

VALUES & PRICING

There is a story, perhaps apocryphal, of Antony and Cleopatra. It seems the cultured Roman, Mark Antony,* fancied himself the world's foremost culinary connoisseur. So confident was he that he challenged the mighty Egyptian Queen, Cleopatra, to a "dinner dare". Whoever could prepare the most expensive meal for two, would be the declared winner. Cleopatra accpeted the challenge and asked to be first.

When Mark Antony arrived at the palace for the expected feast he was led to the elaborately decorated royal dining room. There, he was surprised by the sparsely set table which held only simple place settings for two. Upon being seated, his attention was directed to Cleopatra entering from the kitchen. In her hands she carried a small, covered serving dish and a carving knife. Placing the serving dish in front of her dinner guest, she uncovered it. Revealed was assuredly the largest and finest pearl known to ancient man. So astonished was Antony that he could not utter a word when the Queen then proceeded to slice the gem in two, placing one half onto his plate and the other onto hers. While she chewed on her portion, the humbled general regained his composure and conceded defeat. There was no way that he could outspend her, since pearls were the rarest, most valued gem of the time.

This story illustrates the principal of value, relative to supply and demand. In much of the ancient world, pearls were extremely scarce and highly desired by royalty. Thus, the finest specimens were considered almost priceless. In the South Sea Islands, however, pearls were common enough to be used as a medium of exchange (money) by people.

So, the value of an object is affected by the available supply and the actual demand, both of which vary with location. This principal holds true for cameos as well. Thus, the values listed for cameos in this book are based on "ideal" conditions. That is, a situation where the seller can market a cameo at a time, such as Mother's Day, and a place, such as Beverly Hills, that is ideal for obtaining a top price. These listed values are based on realistic "reference" prices

13

obtained from better auction catalogs and "upscale" jewelry showrooms throughout the United States. In addition, for many of the antique and unusual cameos, the "appraised" value was factored in. This value, which is often used for insurance purposes, is sometimes obtained by calculating the real cost of reproducing the appraised item by hand, from "scratch".

* LATIN SPELLING: Antonius, Marcus

ENGLISH SPELLING: Antony, Mark

REFERENCES:
    WEBSTER'S COLLEGIATE DICTIONARY P1011 Col. 2
    THE ENDURING PAST John Trueman P 216 - 221
    The Roman Successors to Julius Caesar

Shells

PLATE # - S - 1

YEAR - Modern c. 1980's

TYPE OF METAL - Mostly unmounted

TYPE OF SHELL - Cornelian & Sardonyx Helmet

SIZE - Assorted

COMMENTS - This photo was taken at Jewelers of America, summer, 1989 show. These cameos were from the studio of Ginnaro Borriella of Italy, one of the dealers set up at the show. The artists signature (which now appears on the front or obverse of the cameo) on some of the more expensive cameos is visible in this photo.

VALUE - $50 - $2,000

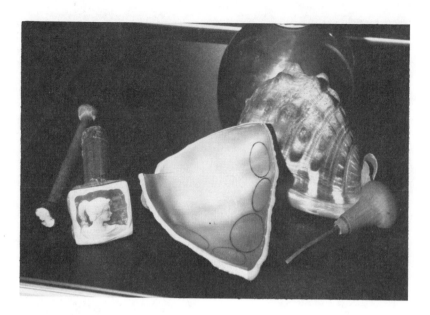

PLATE # - S - 2

YEAR - 1989

TYPE OF SHELL - Sardonyx Helmet

COMMENTS - This photo shows (from right to left), a typical carving tool; the Helmet shell; a cut shell section showing the area from which the cameo shell 'blanks' are cut (note that 'blanks' are cut from the dark portion of the shell, allowing the carver to utilize the darker portion for a contrasting background); two cameos still glued or 'dopped' to dowel-like sticks which the carver can then grasp with one hand while he uses the other to do the carving.

VALUE - $550

Photo is approximately 1/2 actual size. Manufacturer's display at the Jewelers of America Show, July, 1989.

16

PLATE # - S - 3

YEAR - Victorian to WWII

TYPE OF SHELL - Flame Helmets

SIZE - approx. 5" x 3-1/2" each

COMMENTS - Bust of Queen Victoria and Prince Albert on left. On far right scene of Joseph & Mary with Angel holding baby Jesus. (inscription below: 'AVE') 2nd from left: Scene of Venice. In foreground: Victorian lady.

VALUE - $500 - $1,200 each

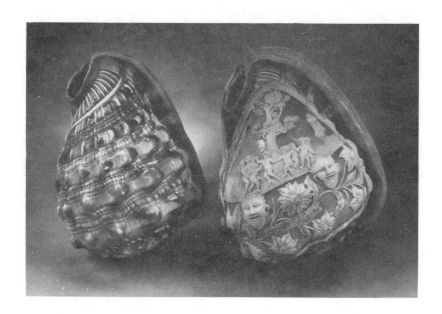

PLATE # - S - 4

YEAR - 1880 (carved shell only)

TYPE OF SHELL - Flame Helmet

SIZE - 6" x 5"

NAME - Dance of Love

COMMENTS - Uncarved shell on left is modern. Note Latin inscription.

VALUE - $1,750

This set once belonged to the American ambassador to Cuba.
See following page

PLATE # - S - 5

YEAR - late 1800's

TYPE OF SHELL - King Helmet

SIZE - 6-1/2" x 5"

NAME - Apollo off to the hunt

COMMENTS - Greek god in wagon being pulled by two lads. Entourage in lead with trumpet player, followed by 3-Graces and two maidens with train.

VALUE - $4,500 for the set

PLATE # - S - 6

YEAR - late 1800's

TYPE OF SHELL - King Helmet

SIZE - 6-1/2" x 5"

NAME - Diana off to the hunt

COMMENTS - Greek goddess in chariot being pulled by two goats. Entourage in lead, two nymphs in rear (including trumpet player)

VALUE - $4,500 for set

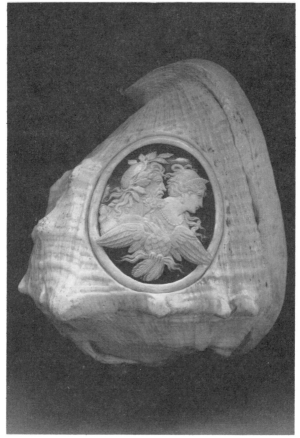

PLATE # - S - 7

YEAR - Early 1900's

TYPE OF SHELL - King Helmet

SIZE - 7" x 6"

NAME - Zeus & Hera

COMMENTS - Museum quality carvings

VALUE - $4,500 for the set

See following page

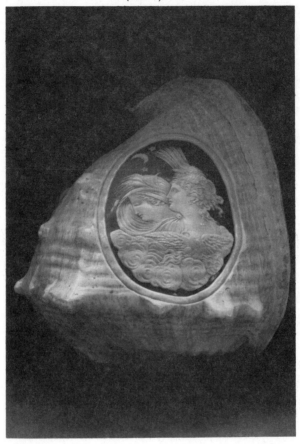

PLATE # - S - 8

YEAR - Early 1900's

TYPE OF SHELL - King Helmet

SIZE - 7" x 6"

NAME - Diana & Aphrodite

COMMENTS - Daughters of Zeus. Zeus, also known as Jupiter is often represented as an eagle in Greek Mythology (Note eagle below busts).

VALUE - $4,500 for the set

PLATE # - S - 9

YEAR - Modern

TYPE OF SHELL - Scotch Bonnet on left, 2 cowry shells in center, Atlantic trampet shell on right

SIZE - 80% of actual

COMMENTS - Simple carvings from Florida and the Caribbean. Probably meant for tourist 'souvenirs'. These are good examples of how almost any shell can be used to carve cameos from. The best shells are thick, multi-layered with contrasting color bands.

VALUE - $2 - $5 each

Female Figures

PLATE # - F - 1

STYLE - Twisted ribbon with twisted wire molding

YEAR - c. 1930

TYPE OF METAL - 10k yellow gold

TYPE OF SHELL - Cornealian Helmet

SIZE - 2-1/4" x 2"

NAME - Greek goddess Venus (Veneve in Italian)

COMMENTS - Museum quality

VALUE - $1,250

PLATE # - F - 2

FRAME STYLE - Plain with intertwined twisted wire. Combination pendant/brooch.

YEAR - c. 1920

TYPE OF METAL - Gold filled

TYPE OF SHELL - Cornelian Helmet

SIZE - 2-1/4" x 1-3/4"

NAME - Greek goddess with sceptre (on left side)

COMMENTS - Note unusual face carved into the shoulder-harness of the robe. The dark spot on the bottom of the frame is the tarnish or oxidation of the metal underneath the gold layer.

VALUE - **$550**

PLATE # - F - 3

FRAME STYLE - Prong-set with Rhinestone 'horseshoe'

YEAR - c. 1900 (Edwardian)

TYPE OF METAL - Gold plated brass

TYPE OF SHELL - Sardonyx Helmet

SIZE - 1-3/8" x 1-1/4"

COMMENTS - It's unusual to find cameo frames set with more than a handful of accent stones (usually pearls).

VALUE - $300

PLATE # - F - 4

FRAME STYLE - 'Prong' - set

YEAR - Victorian

TYPE OF METAL - 14K yellow gold

TYPE OF SHELL - Cornelian Helmet

SIZE - 1" diameter

NAME - Goddess Diana (Artemis)

COMMENTS - Identified by crescent moon adorning her head. Note clever, dual, use of stone mountings (heads), which are holding small, natural pearls (sometimes called seed pearls) and acting as 'prongs' holding the cameo. This size, nearly perfectly circular cameo is quite rare. Most circular cameos are much smaller.

VALUE - $550

PLATE # - F - 5

FRAME STYLE - Unmounted

YEAR - c. 1930

TYPE OF SHELL - Cornelian Helmet

SIZE - 1-1/2" x 2"

NAME - Greek goddess Athena, wearing stylized helmet and necklace

COMMENTS - Signed, fine high relief detail.

VALUE - $200

PLATE # - F - 6

STYLE - Unmounted

YEAR - c. 1890

TYPE OF SHELL - Cornelian Helmet

SIZE - 1-1/4" x 1-1/2"

NAME - Roman Maiden

VALUE - $150

PLATE # - F - 7

STYLE - Unmounted

YEAR - c. 1920's

TYPE OF SHELL - Helmet

SIZE - 1-3/4" x 1-1/4"

NAME - Greco-Roman Lady

COMMENTS - Signed

VALUE - $200

PLATE # - F - 8

FRAME STYLE - Twisted ribbon, pin/pendant

YEAR - Victorian era

TYPE OF METAL - Gold filled

TYPE OF SHELL - Helmet

SIZE - 2-1/4" x 2"

NAME - Woman of Ancient Rome

VALUE - $450

31

PLATE # - F - 9

FRAME STYLE - Twisted ribbon

YEAR - Victorian

TYPE OF METAL - Gold filled

TYPE OF SHELL - Cornelian Helmet

SIZE - 1-3/4" x 1-1/2"

NAME - Mediterranean Woman (Victorian)

COMMENTS - Rectangular cameos are uncommon, especially in larger sizes. This carving is not particularly fine.

VALUE - $300

PLATE # - F - 10

FRAME STYLE - Twisted ribbon brooch

YEAR - Victorian (c. 1850)

TYPE OF METAL - Gold filled

TYPE OF SHELL - Cornelian Helmet

SIZE - 2" x 1-3/4"

NAME - Victorian Woman

COMMENTS - Uncommon shape for a cameo, and an unusual carving in that the artist leaves the white layer in the four corners to frame the bust.

VALUE - $450

PLATE # - F - 11

FRAME STYLE - Unmounted

YEAR - Modern

TYPE OF SHELL - Cornelian Helmet

SIZE - 1-1/4" x 1-3/4"

NAME - Turn of the Century Woman

COMMENTS - Signed. Although not obvious from the photograph, the pearls in the hair are distinctly lighter and whiter than the hair around it. This illustrates the artist's use of the layering of the shell; the white layer being the 'outer prismatic layer' (the outermost layer is scraped away before the artist begins carving).

VALUE - $200

PLATE # - F - 12

YEAR - c. 1920

TYPE OF SHELL - Cornelian Helmet

SIZE - 1-1/2" x 2"

NAME - Gay 90's lady

COMMENTS - Finely detailed, high relief

VALUE - $200

PLATE # - F - 13

FRAME STYLE - Twisted spring-wire brooch with 'safety' pin

ERA - Victorian

TYPE OF METAL - 14k yellow gold

TYPE OF SHELL - Sardonyx Helmet

SIZE - 1-3/4" x 1-1/2" (Pin 1-1/2" long)

NAME - Italian Maiden

COMMENTS - Fine, high-relief carving. Note enlargements detailing frame-design and 'safety' pin.

VALUE - $850

PLATE # - F - 14

YEAR - Modern

TYPE OF METAL - Unmounted

TYPE OF SHELL - Cornelian Helmet

SIZE - 3/4"x1" to 1" x 1-1/4"

COMMENTS - Note varied hair styles. This illustration of modern (post WWII) cameos depicts left and right facing busts. Why are left facing figures much scarcer than right facing ones? Because there are fewer 'lefties' than 'righties'. Left handed carvers find it easier to carve left-facing busts and right handed carvers the opposite.

VALUE - $50 - $150 **each**

PLATE # - F - 15

FRAME STYLE - Filligree

YEAR - 1930's

TYPE OF METAL - Rhodium plated silver

TYPE OF SHELL - Cornelian Helmet

SIZE - 1-3/4" x 2-1/4"

COMMENTS - Note the stylish -- for the 1930's -- beaded hanging hair-piece jewelry.

VALUE - $450

PLATE # - F - 16

FRAME STYLE - Bezel-set

ERA- Late Victorian

TYPE OF METAL - 10k Rose gold

TYPE OF SHELL - Cornelian Helmet

SIZE - 1" x 1-1/4"

COMMENTS - High relief

VALUE - $350

Enlargement showing details of frame & carving.

PLATE # - F - 17

FRAME STYLE - Combination brooch/pendant; filligree-heart and leaf pattern

YEAR - c. 1930

TYPE OF METAL - 14k White gold

TYPE OF SHELL - Cornelian Helmet

SIZE - 1-1/2" x 1-1/4"

NAME - 'Woman Adorned'

COMMENTS - A nice example of a medium-small cameo set with a 6 point (.06 ct.) mine-cut diamond. Note the open-link necklace.

VALUE - $500

PLATE # - F - 18

FRAME STYLE - Filligree-heart brooch/pendant

YEAR - c. 1930's

TYPE OF METAL - 14k white gold

TYPE OF SHELL - Cornelian Helmet

SIZE - 2" x 1-1/2"

NAME - Woman with Diamond Heart Pendant

COMMENTS - Unusual, octahedral (8-sided) shaped cameo. The diamond is a European cut and weighs 5 points (1/20 carat)

VALUE - $950

41

PLATE # - F - 19

STYLE - Unmounted

YEAR - c. 1930's

TYPE OF SHELL - Helmet

SIZE - 1-1/8" x 1-1/2"

NAME - Flowered Lady

COMMENTS - A good example of a fine carving except perhaps, for the tip of the nose.

VALUE - $200

Enlargement showing details of frame and carving.

PLATE # - F - 20

FRAME STYLE - Enamelled bezel-set brooch surrounded by string of moonstone beads.

ERA - Edwardian

TYPE OF METAL - 10k yellow gold

TYPE OF SHELL - Cornelian Helmet

SIZE - 1-1/4" x 1"

NAME - Edwardian Woman

COMMENTS - Signed cameo (signature etched on reverse) Enamel colors are green, black and orange.

VALUE - $650

43

PLATE # - F - 21

FRAME STYLE - Filligree

YEAR - c. 1910

TYPE OF METAL - 14k yellow gold

TYPE OF SHELL - Cornelian Helmet

SIZE - 2-1/2" x 2"

NAME - Edwardian Woman

COMMENTS - Fine carving of an Edwardian woman wearing a pendant set with an 8 point (.08 carat) mine cut diamond.

VALUE - $850

PLATE # - F - 22

FRAME STYLE - Art Nouveau filligree

ERA - 'Flapper' (1920's)

TYPE OF METAL - 14k white gold

TYPE OF SHELL - Cornelian Helmet

SIZE - 2-1/4" x 1-3/4"

COMMENTS - White gold tiara set with 4 pt. mine cut diamond. White gold necklace set with 6 pt. mine cut diamond. Note bow* above tiara and choker necklace, and bow* behind neck. Museum quality. The wearer of this cameo probably mirrored the cameo itself.
*could be fairy wings

See following page
VALUE - $1,500

45

PLATE # - F - 23

COMMENTS - Back-lit photo

See following page

46

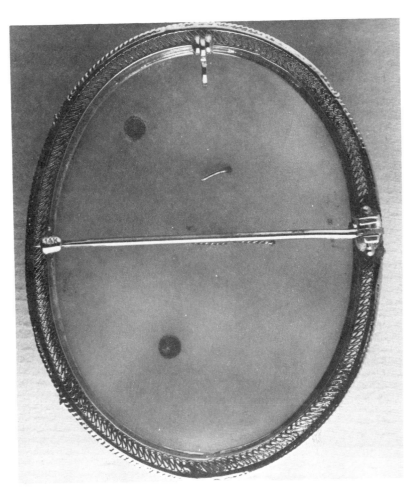

PLATE # - F - 24

COMMENTS - Reverse of cameo showing the pendant mount (at top) in the folded-down position; the 14k hallmark on the pin-clasp; the two tubular bases for the diamond mountings; and the wire-ends (one is partially hidden by the pin) that hold the tiara and the necklace in place. Holes in the cameo had to be carefully drilled to accomodate these wires and tubes.

PLATE # - F - 25

FRAME STYLE - Combination pendant/brooch in ribbon filligree.

YEAR - c. 1920's

TYPE OF METAL - 14k white gold

TYPE OF SHELL - Cornelian Helmet

SIZE - 2-1/2" x 2"

NAME - Diamond-Adorned Woman

COMMENTS - A very graceful carving. The diamonds are European cut and range in size from .06 ct. to .12 ct.

VALUE - $1,500

PLATE # - F - 26

FRAME STYLE - Filligree pin/pendant

YEAR - c. 1920's

TYPE OF METAL - 14k white gold

TYPE OF SHELL - Sardonyx Helmet

SIZE - 2-1/4" x 1-1/2"

NAME - Edwardian Woman

COMMENTS - Note the ten point (1/10 carat) 'mine-cut' diamond brooch that this 'modern' woman of the early 20th century is wearing. Also note octagonal shape. Museum quality.

VALUE - $1,000

PLATE # - F - 27

FRAME STYLE - Combination pendant-brooch with repeating hearts

YEAR - 1930's

TYPE OF METAL - 14k White gold

TYPE OF SHELL - Cornelian Helmet

SIZE - 2" x 1-3/4"

NAME - Flowered Beauty framed by horseshoe

COMMENTS - Uniquely shaped cameo. The artist incorporated the shape into the design of the carving. Museum quality.

VALUE - $1,250

PLATE # - F - 28

STYLE - Filligree

YEAR - c. 1915

TYPE OF METAL - 14k white gold

TYPE OF SHELL - Cornelian Helmet shell

SIZE - 1-1/4" x 2"

COMMENTS - Note diamond shape
From the collection of Briar's Antiques.

VALUE - $550

PLATE # - F - 29

FRAME STYLE - Double twisted wire combination pendant/brooch

YEAR - Modern

TYPE OF METAL - 14k yellow gold

TYPE OF SHELL - Cornelian Helmet

SIZE - 2-1/2" x 2"

NAME - 'Thoroughly Modern Woman'

COMMENTS - Although this is a modern cameo, the woman depicted is probably a 'turn of the century' figure.

VALUE - $850

PLATE # - F - 30

ERA - Art Nouveau c. 1915

TYPE OF METAL - 14k white gold

TYPE OF SHELL - Cornelian Helmet

SIZE - 1-1/4" x 2"

COMMENTS - Set with diamond, 8 pt old mine cut. From the collection of Briars Antiques.

VALUE - $850

Enlargement showing detail
of pendant and object in hand.

PLATE # - F - 31

FRAME STYLE - Art Deco/'Flapper' era pin/pendant

YEAR - 1920's

TYPE OF METAL - 14k white gold

TYPE OF SHELL - Helmet

SIZE - 2" x 1-1/2"

NAME - Flapper lady with finger food.

COMMENTS - Very unusual subject matter. Note the hearts around the frame and the matching heart pendant set with a .05 carat diamond. Also note cracks in upper left quadrant.

VALUE - $650

PLATE # - F - 32

FRAME STYLE - Mixed rope, twisted wire; set with marcasites

YEAR - c. 1946 (date carved on back of cameo)

TYPE OF METAL - Silver

TYPE OF SHELL - Cornelian Helmet

SIZE - 2-1/4" x 2"

NAME - Graduation Girl

COMMENTS - Full frontal view of face is rare. Fine quality carving dated on reverse, 1946. Allegedly from Germany.

VALUE - $750

PLATE # - F - 33

FRAME STYLE - Bezel-set filligree, combination pendant/brooch.

YEAR - c. 1930's

TYPE OF METAL - 14K White gold

TYPE OF SHELL: Cornelian Helmet

SIZE - 2" x 1-3/8"

NAME - 'Flower Framed Woman'

COMMENTS - A well executed octagonal cameo carving. The carved frame on the cameo itself almost seems to eliminate any need for additional framing. Obviously, the original owner disagreed.

VALUE - $850

PLATE # - F - 34

STYLE - Modern brooch/pendant combo

ERA - Post WWI

TYPE OF METAL - 14k yellow gold

TYPE OF SHELL - Sardonyx Helmet

SIZE - 1-1/4" x 1-3/4"

NAME - Innocence

COMMENTS - High relief carving.

VALUE - $550

PLATE # - F - 35

STYLE - Two-sided Pendant Locket. One side set with the cameo, the other set with flat Cornelian cabachon.

YEAR - Early 20th century

TYPE OF METAL - Gold filled

TYPE OF SHELL - Sardonyx Helmet

FRAME SIZE - 7/8" x 5/8"

NAME - Classic Bust of Woman

COMMENTS - Very fine high relief carving. It's extremely rare to find such small lockets set with a shell cameo, because of the stress and wear placed on the cameo when opening and closing the locket. Although the locket shows signs of wear, the cameo appears in nearly perfect condition.

VALUE: $450

PLATE # - F- 36

FRAME STYLE - Modern-customized wire design

YEAR - Modern

TYPE OF METAL - 14k yellow gold

TYPE OF SHELL - Cornelian Helmet

SIZE - 2-3/4" x 2-1/4"

NAME - Sisters

COMMENTS - Large horizontal cameo. Most cameos have a longer vertical dimension than horizontal one.

VALUE - $850

PLATE # - F - 37

STYLE - Link bracelet

YEAR - Modern (Post WWII)

TYPE OF METAL - Gold filled (yellow)

TYPE OF SHELL - Queen (pink) Conch

FRAME SIZE - (each cameo) 1/4" x 5/8"

COMMENTS - Bracelet is 6" long. These are the smallest cameos we have seen. The relative size is apparent in the photo of the bracelet (containing 6 cameos) on top of a one-hundred dollar bill. The quality of the carvings is not particularly good, which is to be expected, given the 'miniature' size of these cameos.

VALUE - $250

1   2   3   4

PLATE # - F - 38

STYLE - Bezel set stick-pins

YEAR - Pre-WWII

TYPE OF METAL - 1) 14k yellow gold 2) Gold filled 3) Gold-plate
4) 10k yellow gold

TYPE OF SHELL - 1 & 4) Cornelian Helmet 2) Pink Conch 3) Molded
pink plastic

CAMEO SIZES - 3/8" x 1/2" to 3/8" x 3/4"

COMMENTS - These are typical examples of the cameos used in stickpins
from the early to mid-1900's.

VALUE - $25 - $150

61

PLATE # - F - 39

STYLES - Assorted

YEAR - Pre-WWII

TYPE OF METAL - Rectangular - 14K White gold; Ovals - Sterling & Coin Silver

TYPE OF SHELL - Sardonyx and Cornelian Helmet

SIZE - All 3 are approximately 1-1/8" x 1-3/8"

COMMENTS - At left: Greek goddess playing lyre. The enlarged photos show the details of the profile and the frame.

VALUE - 14K - $650
Marcasite - $350
Bust left - $250

Details of frames - see next page

Details cont'd. from previous page

PLATE # - F - 40

STYLE - Bezel-set screwback earrings

YEAR - Early 1900's - Modern

TYPE OF METAL - Sterling silver & gold filled

TYPE OF SHELL - Cornelian and Sardonyx Helmet

CAMEO SIZE - 5/16" x 7/16" - 1/2" diameter

COMMENTS - The pair of earrings with the double cameos are depicting either a variation on the popular theme of 'Rebecca at the Well' or 'before' and 'after' scenes of an unmarried young maiden above and the housebound pregnant (?) wife below.

VALUE - $100 - $450

PLATE # - F - 41

STYLE - Bezel & Prong-set brooches

ERA - Victorian

TYPE OF METAL - Gold plated over base-metal

TYPE OF SHELL - Cornelian Helmet

SIZE - 1-3/8" x 1-5/8" - 2-1/2" x 2"

NAME - 'Profiles of Victorian Women'

COMMENTS - These finely carved women are especially noteworthy in that the carver utilized an additional, darker layer of the shell, to 'highlight' the women's hair.

VALUE - $500 each

65

PLATE # - F - 42

STYLE - Assorted pendants and lavaliers (multi-part pendant)

YEAR - Pre-WWII

TYPE OF METAL - 14k white gold and sterling silver

TYPE OF SHELL - Cornelian Helmet

CAMEO SIZE S - 1/2" to 5/8" to 1" x 3/4"

NAME - Assorted Women

COMMENTS - The two 'idealized' women on the left are a sharp contrast to the 'real' women on the right.

VALUE - $150 - $500

Females Modeling

PLATE #- FM-1

COMMENTS - The cameo in the photo is the same as F-17. An illustration of what is traditionally, the most popular way to wear a cameo brooch. (modelled by Darlene Weber) It was not uncommon for aristocratic males of the Renaissance era (and later), who wore frilled and 'lacey' shirts, to don a cameo in the same fashion.

PLATE #- FM-2

STYLE - Combination brooch/pendant.

COMMENTS - In this illustration, the cameo is being worn as a pendant. The loop for the chain, at the top of the cameo is hinged, so that it can be folded back behind the cameo. Then, it could be work as a brooch. (modelled by Darlene Weber)

PLATE #- FM-3

COMMENTS - The cameo in this photo is the same as G-22. This illustration shows another position, just below the collar, that a cameo can be worn in.

PLATE # - FM-4

COMMENTS - The cameo in the photo is the same as F-22. Just as in the previous illustration, a cameo can be worn almost anywhere, although the preferred location has always been -- except for rings -- just below the wearer's face. The explanation for this lies in the fact that most cameos feature a woman's face; the finely carved lines of the cameo best compliment the wearer's facial lines when worn close to the face.

Male Figures

PLATE # - M - 1

FRAME STYLE - Single & double-wire braid; combination brooch/pendant

YEAR - Modern

TYPE OF METAL - 14k yellow gold

TYPE OF SHELL - Cornelian Helmet

FRAME SIZE - 1-1/4" x 1"

NAME - Modern Romeo & Juliet

COMMENTS - Cameo is signed on reverse.

VALUE - $450

PLATE # - M - 2

FRAME STYLE - Filligree

YEAR - c. 1920

TYPE OF SHELL - Cornelian Helmet

SIZE - 1-3/4" x 1-1/2"

NAME - Edwardian Couple

COMMENTS - Style of dress is combination early medieval and classical Greco-Roman. Museum quality.

VALUE - $1,200

PLATE # - M - 2A

STYLE - Bezel-set brooch

ERA - Victorian

TYPE OF METAL - 14K yellow gold

TYPE OF SHELL - Cornelian helmet

FRAME SIZE - 1-3/4" x 1-5/8" - 1'1/2" x 1-1/4"

NAME - 'Renaissance Couple' (The male figure could be Shakespeare)

COMMENTS - Although these two cameos were not found together, they do seem to belong to each other. The artist's use of a darker layer of the shell for highlighting seems similar in both cameos; and the frames, although different in style are from the same era.

VALUE - $1,200 / pair

PLATE # - M - 3

STYLE - Pair of cuff links & earrings

YEAR - Post WWII

TYPE OF METAL - Gold filled and sterling silver

TYPE OF SHELL - Cornelian Helmet

FRAME SIZE - 1" x 3/4" and 1/2" diameter

COMMENTS - The cameos used for the cuff links portray a 'masculine' scene, that of a Roman soldier; and the cameos used for the earrings portray a 'feminine' scene, that of a carefree woman.

VALUE - $150 each pair

PLATE # - M - 4

FRAME STYLE - Unmounted

YEAR - c. 1930's

TYPE OF SHELL - Helmet

SIZE - 1" x 7/8"

NAME - Roman soldier

COMMENTS - Note flying phenix engraved in helmet

VALUE - $100

PLATE # - M - 5

STYLE - Unmounted

ERA - Victorian

TYPE OF SHELL - Sardonyx Helmet

SIZE - 2" x 1-1/2"

NAME - German-Austrian Emperor

COMMENTS - Unmounted; some chips and cracks. These will be ground down before remounting. Note how a piece of the cameo 'peeled away' leaving another, visible layer, below.

VALUE - $250

PLATE # - M - 6

FRAME STYLE - Engraved & enamelled and set with natural pearls

YEAR - c. 1900

TYPE OF METAL - 14k yellow gold

TYPE OF SHELL - Sardonyx Helmet

SIZE - 2" x 1-3/4"

NAME - 'Customized Bust'

COMMENTS - Mr. Dickens of Elmera N.Y. Extremely rare to find a full-face cameo of a male figure. Enlargement shows detail on frame. Museum quality.

VALUE - $1,500

PLATE # - M - 7

STYLE - Mediterranean

ERA - Post-Depression

TYPE OF METAL - 12k yellow gold

TYPE OF SHELL - Sardonyx Helmet

SIZE - 1" dia. & 1/2" x 1"

NAME - Roman Father & Sons

COMMENTS - Pendant with chain. From the collection of Briars Antiques.

VALUE - $750

PLATE # - G - 1

FRAME STYLE - Art Nouveau - filligree

YEAR - c. 1930

TYPE OF METAL - White & yellow gold wash over sterling

TYPE OF SHELL - Cornelian Helmet

SIZE - 2-1/4" x 1-3/4"

NAME - Athena

COMMENTS - Athena, the goddess of war wearing a helmet carved with her father Zeus' head. This represents the mythological legend of Athena being born by 'springing' from the head of her father Zeus. Museum quality.

VALUE - $1,100

PLATE # - G - 2

FRAME STYLE - Entwined leaf

YEAR - Georgian (late 18th century)

TYPE OF METAL - 14k yellow gold

TYPE OF SHELL - Cornelian Helmet

SIZE - 3" x 2-3/4"

NAME - 'Aphrodite (Venus) & her Mother (Dione)'

COMMENTS - Very large cameo in very heavy frame. The only detraction is a small crack, visible in the upper left-hand quadrant. Background of shell is turning greyish brown due to age. The frame, which is unusually heavy; the outer edges of the leaves are 'etched' and the design on the stems, engraved. Museum quality. Aphrodite's bird is the dove, depicted here perched on a horn of flowers. This is in keeping with her image as the Goddess of Beauty and Love who adorns herself and the earth alike, with an embroidery of flowers. The circular 'clouds' along the lower border of the cameo, represent, perhaps, the sea-foam from which, later Greek legend reports, Aphrodite arose. In fact, the Greek word Aphros means foam.

VALUE - $3,500

PLATE # - G - 3

STYLE - Ribbon filligree with 1/2 flower at 4 compass points

ERA - Edwardian

TYPE OF METAL - 14k yellow gold

TYPE OF SHELL - Cornelian Helmet

SIZE - 2-3/4" x 2"

NAME - 'Birth of Venus'

COMMENTS - Signature, probably of the owner rather than the artist, crudely scratched onto back surface. Although this scene could be construed as a version of the Ascension of Christ to heaven, it's more likely that of the Greek goddess Venus (Aphrodite) being born. She arises out of the foam to be greeted by her mother, Dione who is about to adorn her with a 'string' of flowers. Accompanying Dione is a torch-bearing winged-cherub. Museum quality.

VALUE - $1,250

PLATE # - G - 4

STYLE - Unmounted

YEAR - c. 1920

TYPE OF SHELL - Conch

FRAME SIZE - 1-1/2" x 2"

NAME - Two Muses with Phoenix

COMMENTS - In mythology, Zeus' nine daughters were known as the Muses because they were all carefree and of one mind. Through song they can make man forget his troubles and just their presence would dispel sorrow and grief.

VALUE - $250

PLATE # - G - 5

FRAME STYLE - Filligree and leaf combination pendant/brooch

YEAR - c. 1930

TYPE OF METAL - 14k white gold

TYPE OF SHELL - Red/Cornelian Helmet

SIZE - 1-3/4" x 1-1/4"

NAME - Three Graces

COMMENTS - In ancient mythology, these daughters of Zeus also known as Splendor, Mirth and Good Cheer, were the embodiment (together) of beauty and grace. This is probably the most popular of the mythological subjects depicted on shell cameos. Here, as in most scenes of the 3 graces, they are seen dancing (probably to the music from Apollo's lyre.)

VALUE - $650

PLATE # - G - 5A

STYLE - Combination pendant-brooch

ERA - Victorian to modern

TYPE OF METAL - 14K yellow gold (large cameo on left) and .800 fine silver (coin silver) cameos in silver.

TYPE OF SHELL - Cornelian Helmet; cameo in gold-Sardonyx Helmet

SIZE - 1-7/8" x 1-1/4" - 1-1/4" x 1"

NAME - 'The Three Graces'

COMMENTS - Far more interpretations of the Three Graces. Many people mistakenly associate these three mythological figures with the Christian concepts of Faith, Hope, and Charity. But the correct concept is of the Greek interpretation of Aglia (Splendor), Euphrosyne (Mirth), and Thalia (Good Cheer).

VALUE - 3 - silver-framed cameos - $350 each
14K gold framed cameo - $650

PLATE # - G - 6

FRAME STYLE - Combination pendant/brooch in plain frame

YEAR - Modern (post WWII)

TYPE OF METAL - 14k yellow gold

TYPE OF SHELL - Cornelian Helmet

SIZE - 2" x 1-1/2"

NAME - 'Aphrodite and Cupid'

COMMENTS - Very fine carving.

VALUE - $850

PLATE # - G - 7

FRAME STYLE - Plain bezel and lip with twisted wire

ERA - Mid-Victorian

TYPE OF METAL - 14k yellow gold

TYPE OF SHELL - Cornelian Helmet

SIZE - 2-1/4" x 2"

NAME - Cupid playing lyre riding lion - note detailed enlargement

COMMENTS - Unusual cameo in simple frame. This is a good example of a two-step or customized purchase. First the customer chose the cameo, and then the style of frame for its mounting. This was a common practice during the 19th century. People would first select a stone and then choose a mounting or frame for it. Sometimes this process was reversed. The same practice applied to selecting pocket watches and their accompanying cases, chains, and fobs.

VALUE -$1,500

PLATE # - G - 8

YEAR - Modern

TYPE OF METAL - Unmounted

TYPE OF SHELL - Sardonyx or Black cameo

SIZE - 1-1/2" x 1-1/8"

NAME - Goddess Hebe watering Zeus/ eagle

COMMENTS - Partial signature etched on reverse. Note the goddess pouring liquid into bowl, from the pitcher she's holding in her left hand.

VALUE - $250

PLATE # - G - 9

FRAME STYLE - Leaf and Floral pattern

ERA - Edwardian

TYPE OF METAL - 14k yellow gold

TYPE OF SHELL - Red Helmet

SIZE - 1-3/4" x 1-1/2"

NAME - Goddess Hebe feeding Zeus' eagle.

COMMENTS - Left facing scene. Goddess is on a cloud. Multiple cracks in shell. Hebe is traditionally known as the goddess of youth, and also plays the role of cupbearer to the gods.

VALUE - $450,

PLATE # - G - 10

STYLE - Unmounted

ERA - Victorian

TYPE OF SHELL - Cornelian Helmet

SIZE - 1-1/4" x 1"

NAME - Goddess racing 4-horse chariot across sky.

COMMENTS - Very high relief. Exceptionally fine detail. Probably was a jewelry box adornment.

VALUE - $250*

*Can be custom mounted in gold - see appendix

PLATE # - G - 11

FRAME STYLE - Frame twisted wire

YEAR - Post 1930's

TYPE OF METAL - 14k yellow gold

TYPE OF SHELL - Cornelian Helmet

SIZE - 2" W x 1-3/4" H

NAME - Greek Goddess in chariot

COMMENTS - Unsigned

VALUE - $500

PLATE # - G - 11A

STYLE - Prong Set Combination Pendant/brooch set with marcasites

YEAR - c. 1930's

TYPE OF METAL - .800 fine silver (coin silver)

TYPE OF SHELL - Cornelian helmet (very dark background)

SIZE - 1-1/2" x 1-1/4"

NAME - 'Helmeted Greek God Standing In Chariot'

COMMENTS - Note that the male figure is nude and the legs appear detached from the torso.

VALUE - $500

PLATE # - G - 12

STYLE - Unmounted

YEAR - Post WWII

TYPE OF SHELL - Helmet

FRAME SIZE - 1-3/4" x 1-1/4"

NAME - Olympian Processional

VALUE - $300

PLATE # - G - 13

FRAME STYLE - Plain with twisted wire inside border

ERA - Victorian

TYPE OF METAL - 14k white gold

TYPE OF SHELL - Pink Conch

SIZE - 3/4" x 1"

NAME - Roman Gladiator in Chariot drawn by two Maidens.

COMMENTS - Because the color of this cameo ranges from white to light pink, there is hardly any contrast between the foreground and the background. This diminishes the overall appeal of the cameo as well as its desirability and value.

VALUE - $350

PLATE # - G - 14

FRAME STYLE - Etruscan

YEAR - c. 1860

TYPE OF METAL - 18k yellow gold

TYPE OF SHELL - Cornelian Helmet

SIZE - 2-3/4" x 1-3/8"

NAME - Greek goddesses picking flowers.

COMMENTS - Frame is large and heavy and in pristine condition. Museum quality.

VALUE - $2500

PLATE # - G - 15

STYLE - Chain link with twisted molding

ERA - Victorian-Greek revival

TYPE OF METAL - 18k yellow gold

TYPE OF SHELL - Sardonyx Helmet

SIZE - 2" x 2-1/2"

NAME - Hercules throwing bull with goddess-head behind

COMMENTS - From the collection of Briar's Antiques.

VALUE - $950

PLATE # - G - 16

FRAME STYLE - Filligree-combination brooch - pendant

YEAR - 1930's

TYPE OF METAL - Rhodium over silver

TYPE OF SHELL - Helmet

SIZE - 2-1/2" x 2"

NAME - Artemis (Diana)

COMMENTS - Moon goddess riding crescent moon. Museum quality.

VALUE - $1,000

PLATE # - G - 17

FRAME STYLE - Tubular brass

YEAR - c. 1930's

TYPE OF METAL - Brass

TYPE OF SHELL - Sardonyx Helmet

SIZE - 2" x 2-1/4"

NAME - Goddess Athena

COMMENTS - In poetry, Athena stands for wisdom, reason, and purity. The owls head on her hip represents wisdom, the scepter represents reason and the chalice represents purity.

VALUE - $450

PLATE # - G - 18

FRAME STYLE - Scalloped

YEAR - c. 1870's

TYPE OF METAL - 14k Victorian rose-gold

TYPE OF SHELL - Cornelian Helmet

SIZE - 2-1/2" x 2-1/4"

NAME - Two Muses

COMMENTS - Frame is shown as is listed value assumes fully restored frame.

VALUE - $1,400

PLATE # - G - 19

FRAME STYLE - Engraved wire and leaves.

ERA - Victorian

TYPE OF METAL - Gold filled (2-color)

TYPE OF SHELL - Sardonyx Helmet

SIZE - 1-1/2" x 3/4" and 3/4" x 1/2"

NAME - Aphrodite dancing with Cupid* (above); Aphrodite playing the Lyre´ (below)

COMMENTS - Top cameo shows horizontal crack that was repaired long ago by filling in with resin.
*Cupid was also known as Eros, the son of Aphrodite.

VALUE - $250

PLATE # - G - 20

FRAME STYLE - Filligree

ERA - Victorian

TYPE OF METAL - 14k yellow gold

TYPE OF SHELL - Helmet

SIZE - 2" w x 2-1/2" h

NAME - 'Eros Serenading Sea Nymphs'

COMMENTS - Signed, from the Collection of Briars Antiques, Olney, Maryland.

VALUE - $1,200

PLATE # - G - 21

FRAME STYLE - Simple bezel with lip

ERA - Victorian

TYPE OF METAL - 14k white gold

TYPE OF SHELL - Sardonyx Helmet

SIZE - 2" x 1-1/2"

NAME - Cupid observing Victim

VALUE - $750

PLATE # - G - 22

FRAME STYLE - Baroque - hand engraved

YEAR - c. 1830

TYPE OF METAL - Gold washed silver

TYPE OF SHELL - Cornelian Helmet

SIZE - 2-1/4" x 1-3/4"

NAME - Cupid with his mother Aphrodite

COMMENTS - Signed. Museum quality ("Ferd")

VALUE - $1,000

PLATE # - G - 23

STYLE - Unframed

YEAR - Post WWII

TYPE OF SHELL - Cornelian Helmet

SIZE - 2-5/8" x 2-1/4"

NAME - Cupid playing harp with mother Aphrodite.

VALUE - $500

PLATE # - G - 24

FRAME STYLE - Combination brooch/pendant, prong-set

YEAR - c. 1930

TYPE OF METAL - .800 silver set with marcasites

TYPE OF SHELL - Helmet

SIZE - approx. 1-3/4" diameter

NAME - Eros (Cupid) kneeling over Psyche (the Soul)

COMMENTS - Circular-fine carving. In this mythological scene, the grown-up Cupid (Eos) son of Aphrodite (Venus) is leaning over his love, the mortal Psyche. Eros appears to be reaching for an arrow from the quiver attached to his back. According to the legend Eros is about to prick Psyche with the point of his arrow in order to wake her from the deep sleep that his jealous mother, Venus, had indirectly induced. Eros then declared his marriage to Psyche demanded of Jupiter, the father of the Gods, that she be made immortal. Jupiter granted the request, since this solution satisfied all parties. Venus would no longer have cause to be jealous now that her son had a suitable bride (a goddess), nor would her daughter-in-law represent mortal, earthly competition for Venus. Now it had become incontravertible that Love could not exist without the Soul, and the Soul could not exist with Love. That union would last forever!

VALUE - $650

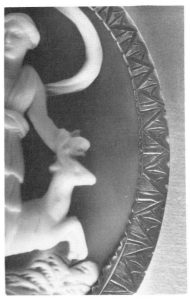

PLATE # - G - 25

FRAME STYLE - Solid back (see photo) brooch with scalloped-edged bezel and hand engraved frame

ERA - Early Victorian

TYPE OF METAL - Silver - unmarked (Probably coin-silver)

TYPE OF SHELL - Sardonyx Helmet

SIZE - 2-1/4" x 1-7/8"

NAME - The Young Huntress

COMMENTS - Museum quality. The scene is probably a depiction of the goddess, Diana, with a 'live' trophy. Diana is dressed as a mortal, so as to hide her true identity.

VALUE - $950

See following page

105

PLATE # - G - 26

COMMENTS - Back of cameo frame showing pin style and solid back.

See following page for details

Details from previous page

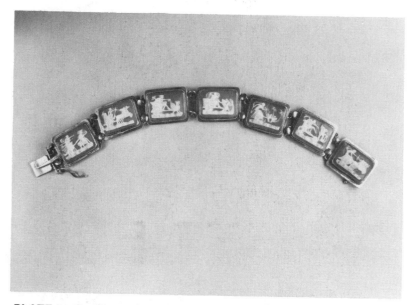

PLATE # - G - 27

STYLE - Bezel-set, linked bracelet

YEAR - Post WWII

TYPE OF METAL - .800 fine silver (coin-silver) with 18k yellow gold twisted inside border.

TYP E OF SHELL - Cornelian Helmet

FRAME SIZE - 5/8" x 7/8" each

NAME - '7 Days of the Week'

COMMENTS - Photo is reduced to about 80% of actual size. This is a variation on the theme of seven different gods and goddesses each representing a different day of the week as follows: (from left to right) Monday: Diana, the goddess of hunting and chastity; Tuesday: Mars, the god of war; Wednesday: Mercury, the god of trade and protector of thieves; Thursday: Jupiter, the father of the gods; Friday: Venus, the goddess of love and beauty; Saturday: Saturnus, the god of agriculture; Sunday: Apollo, god of the sun, art and medicine.

VALUE - $1,500

Religious Scenes

PLATE # - R - 1

FRAME STYLE - Twisted ribbon & leaf

ERA - Edwardian

TYPE OF METAL - Gold filled

TYPE OF SHELL - Sardonyx Helmet

SIZE - 2" x 1-3/4"

NAME - 'Rebecca At The Well'

COMMENTS - Common variation on a common theme, except that this cameo is carved in high-relief and set in an exquisite frame.

VALUE - $550

PLATE # - R - 2

FRAME STYLE - Twisted

ERA - Early Victorian

TYPE OF METAL - Pinchbeck (Alloy of zinc and copper that looks like gold)

TYPE OF SHELL - Cornelian Helmet

SIZE - 2-1/2" x 2"

NAME - Early Christian Family Scene

COMMENTS - Original owner scratched initials on back of cameo. Note banner hanging from cross. Perhaps a banner of mourning. Rare religious scene.

VALUE - $850

PLATE # - R - 3

FRAME STYLE - Twisted wires surrounding bezel

ERA - Edwardian

TYPE OF METAL - 10k Yellow and Rose gold

TYPE OF SHELL - Cornelian Helmet

SIZE - 2" x 1-3/4"

NAME - King David Playing Harp

COMMENTS - This cameo is much less worn than it appears in the enlarged photo. Rare, Biblical scene.

VALUE - $850

PLATE # - R - 4

FRAME STYLE - Twisted wire and hand engraved solid frame.

YEAR - c. 1920's

TYPE OF METAL - 14k yellow gold

TYPE OF SHELL - Cornelian Helmet

SIZE - 2" x 1-3/4"

COMMENTS - Haloed woman playing lyre. Note the enlargements showing the detail in the cameo and the detail of the frame design.

See following page for details   **VALUE - $950**

Details continued from previous page

PLATE # - R - 5

FRAME STYLE - Mediterranean

ERA - Early 1900's

TYPE OF METAL - Coin silver

TYPE OF SHELL - Fountain conch

SIZE - 1-1/2" x 3/4"

NAME - Religious figure-head

COMMENTS - Note natural pinholes. Perhaps a representation of a saint or even Christ.

VALUE - $250

PLATE # - R - 6

FRAME STYLE - Combination pendant-brooch; double-edged outer frame enclosing ribbon filligree; double-leafed at 4 compass points.

ERA - Edwardian

TYPE OF METAL - 14k yellow gold

TYPE OF SHELL - Cornelian Helmet

SIZE - 2" x 1-3/4"

NAME - 'The Ascension'

COMMENTS - Whether or not this carving is a romantic depiction of the Ascension of Christ is open to question. Some aspects of the scene argue against this designation. Most notable is that the figures seem to be reversed. The angel, who appears to be a male, is helping the alleged Christ who appears to be a female (adorned with fairy wings), to ascend.

It is just as likely that this scene has its roots in Greek mythology* and as in medieval times, when cameos were especially popular among the Christian clergy, the owners (including the jewelers who sold cameos) attached appropriate religious explanations to the cameo scene. This allowed the wearer -- especially members of the clergy -- to avoid the appearance of involvement with pagan mythology.

*Probably Eros ascending to heaven with Psyche, his wife.

PLATE # - R - 7

FRAME STYLE - Bezel set combination brooch/pendant

ERA - Post WWII

TYPE OF METAL - Sterling Silver (hallmarked, 975)

TYPE OF SHELL - Sardonyx Helmet

FRAME SIZE - 2" x 1-1/2"

NAME - 'Eve In the Garden of Eden'

COMMENTS - This is another example of a scene that is probably mythological (note the 'fairy' wings) being represented as -- and in the public's mind accepted as -- Biblical. What appear to be scuff marks on the white surfaces of the cameo are actually natural imperfections.

VALUE - $550

PLATE # - R - 8

STYLE - Prong-set pendant

YEAR - c. 1930's

TYPE OF METAL - 14K yellow gold

TYPE OF SHELL - Cornelian Helmet

FRAME SIZE - 1-1/2" x 2"

NAME - 'Adam & Eve Fleeing the Garden of Eden'

COMMENTS - Fine Carving

VALUE: $850

Other (miscellaneous) subjects

PLATE # - O - 1

FRAME STYLE - Braided

ERA - Late Victorian

TYPE OF METAL - Yellow gold filled

TYPE OF SHELL - Cornelian Helmet

SIZE - 1-3/4" x 2"

NAME - Flower bouquet

COMMENTS -   Flowers are one of the more popular non-figural themes utilized by cameo artists.

VALUE - $250

PLATE # - O - 2

FRAME STYLE - Unmounted

YEAR - Late 1800's

TYPE OF SHELL - Sardonyx Helmet

SIZE - 1-3/4" x 1-3/4"

NAME - Bouquet of Garden Flowers

COMMENTS - In ancient mythology flowers were regarded as creations of the gods. All beautiful things were said to have come from the gods.

VALUE - $300

PLATE # - O - 3

STYLE - Unmounted

YEAR - Modern

TYPE OF SHELL - Cornelian Helmet

SIZE - 1" x 1-1/4"

NAME - Smiling Steed

COMMENTS - Animals by themselves were not particularly popular subject matters for cameo carvers in the past. This carving of a horse's head was one of several similar carvings purchased from an upstate N.Y. stone dealer's inventory.

VALUE - $100

PLATE # - O - 4

FRAME STYLE - Prong-set pendant

YEAR - Modern

TYPE OF METAL - 14k yellow gold

TYPE OF SHELL - Cornelian Helmet

FRAME SIZE - 1" Diameter

NAME - 'Capricorn (goat)'

COMMENTS - Although the signs of the Zodiac are a popular theme in jewelry, it's rare to find them in cameos. The frame is made of heavy gauge gold.

VALUE - $550

PLATE # - O - 5

FRAME STYLE - Twisted ribbon

YEAR - Victorian

TYPE OF SHELL - Sardonyx Helmet

TYPE OF METAL - Gold filled

SIZE - 1-1/2" x 1-7/8"

NAME - 'Women at the Village Mill'

COMMENTS - Horizontal oval cameos are uncommon. This is a fine example of an outdoor scene.

VALUE - $500

PLATE # - O - 6

STYLE - Cameo-locket combination

ERA - Victorian

TYPE OF METAL - Heavy gold filled

TYPE OF SHELL - Cornelian Helmet

SIZE - 2-1/2" x 2"

NAME - 'Young Maiden Awaiting Her Lover'

COMMENTS - This cameo is set in a frame that swivels on its vertical axis within another frame to reveal a locket on the other side. The locket probably held a lock of hair or photo of the woman's (owner's) lover. Frame and cameo are in excellent condition.

VALUE - $750

See following page

PLATE # - O - 7

COMMENTS - Locket in reverse position.

See following page

PLATE # - O - 8

COMMENTS - Locket in reverse position.

See following page

PLATE # - O - 9

COMMENTS - Cameo in reverse position.

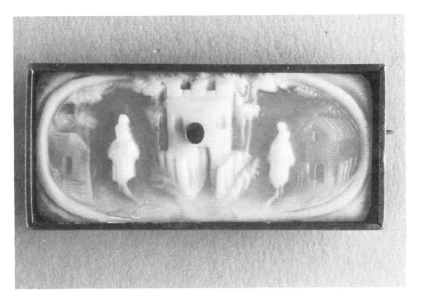

PLATE # - O - 10

STYLE - Brooch (note rivet holding cameo in frame)

YEAR - Victorian

TYPE OF METAL - Gold filled

TYPE OF SHELL - Cornelian Helmet

SIZE - 5/8" x 1-1/2"

NAME - Village Woman or possible variation of Rebecca At The Well

COMMENTS - Extremely rare, double/mirror scene carved on a rectangular cameo.

VALUE - $850

PLATE # - O - 11

STYLES- Bezel-set combination pendant/brooch

ERA - Victorian

TYPE OF METAL - 14K yellow gold

TYPE OF SHELL - Sardonyx Helmet

SIZE - 1-5/8" x 1-7/8"

NAME - 'Village Scene'

COMMENTS - Unusual village scene depicting a horse at a trough. Note the 'open' door to the left of the horse, and the woman, head on hand, waiting on the porch. Large crack in right hand quadrant.

VALUE - $350

PLATE # - O - 12

STYLE - Bezel-set pendant

YEAR - Post WWII

TYPE OF METAL - Coin silver

TYPE OF SHELL - Undetermined

CAMEO SIZE - 3/4" diameter

NAME - Mount Vesuvius

COMMENTS - This cameo shell exhibits 3 layers of brown (in different shades) above an all white background.

VALUE - $250

PLATE # - O - 13

FRAME STYLE - Bezel-set brooch; heavy twisted wire

YEAR - Pre- WWII

TYPE OF METAL - Gold wash over silver

TYPE OF SHELL - Cornelian Helmet

SIZE - 1-5/8" x 1-1/4"

NAME - Village Harbor

COMMENTS - Cameo is signed on reverse. Although the quality of the carving is ordinary, the scene is unusual.

VALUE - $350

PLATE # - O - 14

FRAME STYLE - Lace pattern, bezel-set brooch

YEAR - Pre-WWII

TYPE OF METAL - Gold wash over silver

TYPE OF SHELL - Cornelian Helmet

SIZE - 2-3/8" x 1-7/8"

NAME - 'Village On A Hillside'

COMMENTS - A wonderful carving. Note, natural imperfections in the background to the left of the tree.

VALUE - $650

PLATE # - O - 15

STYLE - Combination pendant/brooch, bezel-set surrounded by natural pearls

YEAR - c. 1920's

TYPE OF METAL - Gold-filled

TYPE OF SHELL - Cornelian Helmet

SIZE - 1-1/2" x 1-1/4"

NAME - 'Girl With Her Dog'

COMMENTS - Excellent, bold, high relief carving with 'soft' background. Note enclosed back (see attached photo of reverse)

See following page for reverse details   **VALUE - $1,000**

PLATE # - O - 15A

Continued from previous page

PLATE # - O - 16

STYLE - Earring

YEAR - Victorian

TYPE OF METAL - Gold Filled

TYPE OF SHELL - Sardonyx Shell

SIZE - 1" x 7/8"

NAME - Woman at Village Fence

COMMENTS - Possibly a variation of 'Rebecca At The Well'. This is a fair sized earring.

VALUE - $250

PLATE # - O - 17

STYLE - Bezel-set brooch with twisted wire and twisted ribbon.

YEAR - Victorian

TYPE OF SHELL - Cornelian Helmet

SIZE - 1-3/4" x 1-3/8"

NAME - 'Woman In Village'

COMMENTS - Unusual rectangular-rounded edges shape.

VALUE: $350

PLATE # - O - 18

STYLE - Bezel-set brooch

YEAR - c. 1920's

TYPE OF METAL - Gold filled

TYPE OF SHELL - Cornelian Helmet

SIZE - 2" x 1-5/8"

NAME - 'Woman Holding Birdhouse'

COMMENTS - This is an excellent carving and an unusual scene. Note the bird about to fly into the 'birdhouse'.

VALUE - $750

Natural, Non-shell Cameos

PLATE # - N - 1

FRAME STYLE - Bezel-set brooch

ERA - Mid-Victorian

TYPE OF METAL - Gold-plated

TYPE - 2-piece stone cameo

SIZE - 1-1/2" Diameter

NAME - Bust of Greek Goddess

COMMENTS - The bust is carved from one piece of layered (banded) stone and glued to the background stone, which is also layered.

VALUE - $500

PLATE # - N - 2

FRAME STYLE - Custom engraved and etched

ERA - Victorian

TYPE OF METAL - Gold filled

TYPE - Stone (onyx) cameo, sometimes called a 'black' cameo.

SIZE - 1-1/8" x 7/8"

NAME - 'Black Cameo'

COMMENTS - The use of the black cameo suggests that this pin might be of the 'mourning jewelry' genre, popularized during the second half of the 19th century by the wearing of black following the death of Queen Victoria's husband, Prince Albert.

VALUE - $250

PLATE # - N - 3

STYLE - Lavalier (multi-piece) set with marcasites.

ERA - Edwardian

TYPE OF METAL - Sterling Silver

TYPE - Stone Cameo

SIZE - 3" x 3/4"

NAME - Contemporary Woman's Bust

VALUE - (with sterling silver chain) $375

PLATE # - N - 4

STYLE - Hinged bangle bracelet

ERA - Victorian

TYPE OF METAL - Heavy gold filled

TYPE OF SHELL - Stone cameo

FRAME SIZE - 1" x 3/4"; bracelet is approximately 2-1/4" in diameter

NAME - 'Roman Gladiator with Shield'

VALUE - $550

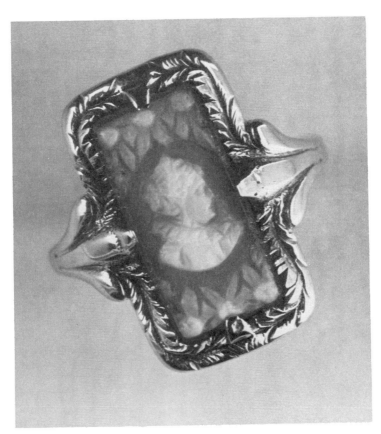

PLATE # - N - 5

STYLE - Ring

ERA - Edwardian

TYPE OF METAL - 14k yellow gold

SHELL - Stone Cameo

SIZE - 1/2" x 3/4"

NAME - Elizabethan Woman

COMMENTS - Since the tradition of stone cameos predates, considerably, that of shell cameos, its more common to find stone cameo carvings of figures in Renaissance and pre-costume. The photo enlargement caused the loss of detail and sharpness in the picture.

VALUE -$500

PLATE # - N - 6

FRAME STYLE - Scalloped pendant

YEAR - Early 1900's

TYPE OF METAL - 14k Gold (outer frame and oval insert with diamond on reverse, only) and gold plate.

TYPE - Stone Cameo

SIZE - 2-1/4" x 1"

NAME - Ancient Roman Military Officer

COMMENTS - A most unusual, probably unique, 'conglomeration' of a stone cameo set in a bezel which in turn is set in a 'scalloped' carved piece of cornelian, set in a 14k yellow gold frame which is adorned, at the top, with a blue and white enamelled upside-down 'fleur' and adorned on the back with what appears to be the top portion of a shirt stud in 14k gold with diamond inset.

VALUE - $650

See following page

PLATE # - N - 7

COMMENTS - Back-side of stone cameo 'conglomeration'

Continued from previous page

PLATE # - N - 8

STYLE - Bezel-set brooch with wire ribbon border.

YEAR - Post WWII

TYPE OF METAL - 14k yellow gold

TYPE - Lava

SIZE - 1-1/4" x 1"

NAME - 'Cupid Playing Lyre'

COMMENTS - Extremely high-relief carving (up to 3/8" from background to high point of foreground) -- looks more like a 3-dimensional sculpture. Museum quality.

See following page   **VALUE - $750**

PLATE # - N - 8a

Continued from previous page

PLATE # - N - 9

FRAME STYLE - Enamelled, bezel-set pin

YEAR - Pre-WWII

TYPE OF METAL - Silver (probably coin silver)

TYPE - Ivory

FRAME SIZE - 1-1/2" x 1-1/4"

NAME - 'Oriental Woman Bearing Fruit'

COMMENTS - Very high relief (deep) carving. (1/8" and more from background to high points of foreground.) Enamel colors are green, blue, and purple.

VALUE - $450

146

PLATE # - N - 10

STYLE - Ring

ERA - Edwardian

TYPE OF METAL - 14K yellow gold

TYPE - Stone Cameo

SIZE - 3/4" x 1/2"

NAME - Elizabethan Woman

COMMENTS - A very fine stone-cameo sculpture.

VALUE - $650

PLATE # - N - 11

YEAR - Pre- WWII

TYPE OF METAL - Unmounted

TYPE OF SHELL - Stone Cameo

SIZE - 3/4" x 1/2"

COMMENTS - This double profile sculpture of a helmeted Greek god and goddess exhibits 3 different color-layers. This theme is very common in small stone cameos that were mounted in men's rings.

VALUE - $100

PLATE # - N - 12

STYLE - Pin

YEAR - Pre-WWII

TYPE OF METAL - 10K yellow gold

TYPE OF SHELL - Stone Cameo

SIZE - 3/4" x 1/2"

COMMENTS - Unusual sculpting of letters representing some fraternal organization.

VALUE - $250

PLATE # - N - 13

STYLE - Ring set with marcasites

YEAR - c. 1930's

TYPE OF METAL - .800 fine silver (coin silver)

TYPE OF SHELL - Black Abalone

SIZE - 5/8" x 7/8"

COMMENTS - Lovely carving of a Mediterranean woman in two-toned abalone. Abalone is a common dish-shaped shell that is found all over the world. The inside of the shell is noteworthy for its iridescent shades. This feature is what makes it popular for use in jewelry. Abalone is not usually found with distinctive enough contrasting-colored 'banding' or thick layering to be widely used for cameos.

VALUE - $250

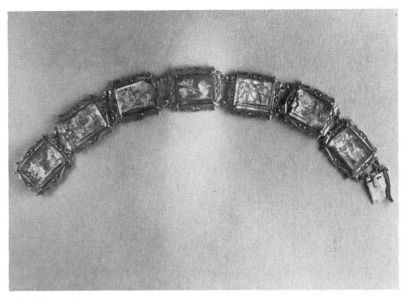

PLATE # - N - 14

STYLE - Bracelet set with marcasites

YEAR - 1930's

TYPE OF METAL - .800 fine silver (coin silver)

TYPE OF SHELL - Black Abalone

FRAME SIZE - 5/8" x 7/8" each

NAME - '7 Days of the Week' (see G-27 for detailed comments)

COMMENTS - Bracelet is 7" long

VALUE - $1,000

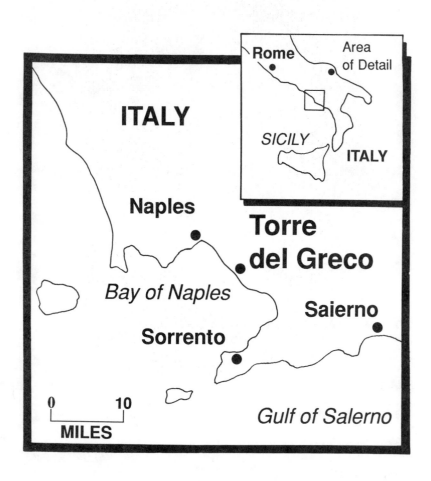

CAMEO PRODUCTIONS CENTERS
OF ITALY

Area
of Detail

Rome

ITALY

SICILY

ITALY

Naples

Torre
del Greco

Bay of Naples

Saierno

Sorrento

0   10

MILES

Gulf of Salerno

Imitation Cameos

PLATE # - I - 1

STYLE - No frame - pin glued on back

ERA - Edwardian

TYPE OF METAL - Brass

TYPE - Imitation. Made of bakelite.

SIZE - 1" x 1-3/4"

NAME - Woman of Ancient Greece

COMMENTS - Molded. Note lack of carving lines and 'mushy' look typical of 'fake' cameos.

VALUE - $25

PLATE # - I - 2

YEAR - 1900 - present

TYPE OF METAL - Pot metal

TYPE - 'Imitation' cameos made of assorted plastics, glass and painted ceramics.

SIZE - 2-1/4" x 1-3/4" 1-1/4" x 1"

COMMENTS - The three 'fake' cameos on the bottom row are quite attractive and look very real.

VALUE - $5 - $50

PLATE # - I - 3

YEAR - 1990

FRAME TYPE OF METAL - White metal

TYPE - Lucite and slate

SIZE - 2" x 2-1/2"

NAME - The Black Cameo®

COMMENTS - This cameo was created by Coreen Simpson of N.Y. City for 'today's African-American woman'

VALUE - $120

BROOCHES AND BAR PINS

14Kt. White Gold and Platinum Top

10Kt. White Gold and Platinum Top

14Kt. and 10Kt. White Gold

Attractive Designs; Good Weight. Finely Pierced and Finished. All Pins have Safety Catches. Illustrations actual size

Prices Subject to Wholesale Discounts. See Page 2.

AJ3119 14 Kt. **$11.80** White Gold, pierced and chased. Special value.

AJ3120 14 Kt. **$28.50** White Gold, heavy weight. Fine White Diamond.

AJ3121 14 Kt. **$29.50** White Gold, pierced filigree. Fine White Diamond.

AJ3122 14 Kt. **$26.50** White Gold, pierced filigree. Fine White Diamond.

AJ3123 10 Kt. **$22.80** White Gold, modernistic design. Fine White Diamond.

Carnelian Cameos shown above are selected quality, finely carved. All pins fitted with safety catches and pendant rings to attach to chains.

PLATE #-C-1
Excerpt from 1930's Jewelry Catalog

156

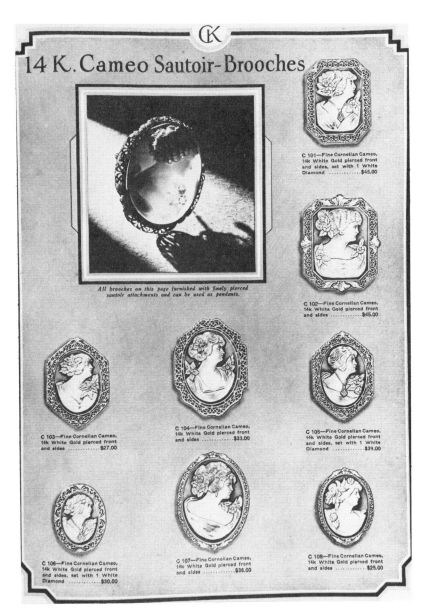

14 K. Cameo Sautoir-Brooches

All brooches on this page furnished with finely pierced sautoir attachments and can be used as pendants.

C 101—Fine Cornelian Cameo, 14k White Gold pierced front and sides, set with 1 White Diamond $45.00

C 102—Fine Cornelian Cameo, 14k White Gold pierced front and sides $45.00

C 103—Fine Cornelian Cameo, 14k White Gold pierced front and sides $27.00

C 104—Fine Cornelian Cameo, 14k White Gold pierced front and sides $33.00

C 105—Fine Cornelian Cameo, 14k White Gold pierced front and sides, set with 1 White Diamond $39.00

C 106—Fine Cornelian Cameo, 14k White Gold pierced front and sides, set with 1 White Diamond $30.00

C 107—Fine Cornelian Cameo, 14k White Gold pierced front and sides $36.00

C 108—Fine Cornelian Cameo, 14k White Gold pierced front and sides $25.00

PLATE #-C-2
Excerpt from 1930's Jewelry Catalog

Cameo Brooches

C 109—Fine Cornelian Cameo, 10k White Gold pierced mounting $16.50

C 110—Fine Cornelian Cameo, 10k White Gold pierced mounting $21.00

C 111—Fine Cornelian Cameo, 10k White Gold pierced mounting, set with 1 White Diamond $33.00

C 112—Fine Cornelian Cameo, 10k White Gold pierced mounting, set with 1 White Diamond $27.00

C 113—Fine Cornelian Cameo, 10k White Gold pierced mounting $28.50

C 114—Fine Cornelian Cameo, 10k White Gold pierced mounting $15.00

C 115—Fine Cornelian Cameo, 10k White Gold pierced mounting $14.00

C 116—Fine Cornelian Cameo, 10k White Gold pierced mounting, set with 1 White Diamond............$27.00

C 117—Fine Cornelian Cameo, 10k White Gold pierced mounting, set with 1 White Diamond $24.00

C 118—Fine Cornelian Cameo, 10k White Gold pierced mounting, set with 1 White Diamond $25.50

C 119—Fine Cornelian Cameo, 10k White Gold pierced mounting $20.00

C 120—Fine Cornelian Cameo, 10k White Gold pierced mounting $12.00

PLATE #-C-3
Excerpt from 1930's Jewelry Catalog

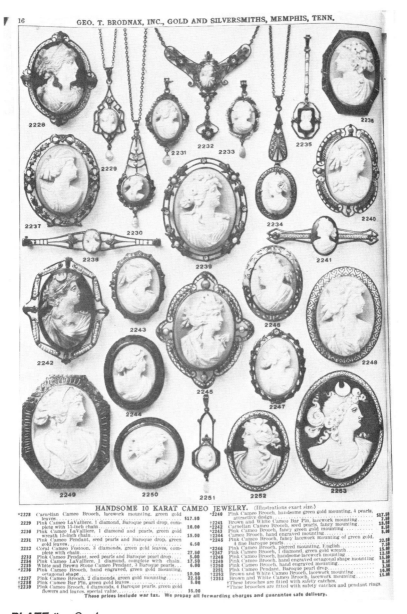

HANDSOME 10 KARAT CAMEO JEWELRY. (Illustrations exact size.)

*2228	Carnelian Cameo Brooch, lacework mounting, green gold leaves	$17.50	
2229	Pink Cameo LaValliere, 1 diamond, Baroque pearl drop, complete with 15-inch chain	10.00	
2230	Pink Cameo LaValliere, 1 diamond and pearls, green gold wreath 15-inch chain	15.00	
2231	Pink Cameo Pendant, seed pearls and Baroque drop, green gold leaves	6.50	
2232	Coral Cameo Festoon, 3 diamonds, green gold leaves, complete with chain	27.50	
2233	Pink Cameo Pendant, seed pearls and Baroque pearl drop	5.00	
2234	Pink Cameo LaValliere, 1 diamond, complete with chain	17.50	
2235	White and Brown Stone Cameo Pendant, 3 Baroque pearls	6.00	
*2236	Pink Cameo Brooch, hand engraved, green gold mounting, octagonal shape	10.00	
†2237	Pink Cameo Brooch, 2 diamonds, green gold mounting	22.50	
†2238	Pink Cameo Bar Pin, green gold leaves	5.00	
†2239	Pink Cameo Brooch, 4 diamonds, 4 Baroque pearls, green gold flowers and leaves, special value	35.00	
*†2240	Pink Cameo Brooch, handsome green gold mounting, 4 pearls, attractive design	$17.50	
†2241	Brown and White Cameo Bar Pin, lacework mounting	7.50	
*†2242	Carnelian Cameo Brooch, seed pearls, fancy mounting	18.50	
*†2243	Pink Cameo Brooch, fancy green gold mounting	8.50	
*†2244	Cameo Brooch, hand engraved mounting	9.50	
*†2245	Pink Cameo Brooch, fancy lacework mounting of green gold, 4 fine Baroque pearls	22.50	
†2246	Pink Cameo Brooch, pierced mounting, English	7.50	
*†2247	Pink Cameo Brooch, 1 diamond, green gold wreath	15.00	
†2248	Pink Cameo Brooch, handsome lacework mounting	13.50	
†2249	Pink Cameo Brooch, hand engraved octagonal shape mounting	16.00	
†2250	Pink Cameo Brooch, hand engraved mounting	8.50	
†2251	Pink Cameo Pendant, Baroque pearl drop	3.50	
†2252	Brown and White Cameo Brooch, lacework mounting	16.00	
†2253	Brown and White Cameo Brooch, lacework mounting	15.00	

*These brooches are fitted with safety catches and pendant rings.

These prices include war tax. We prepay all forwarding charges and guarantee safe delivery.

PLATE # - C - 4

COMMENTS- Excerpt from a 1919 catalog. Note that the illustrations are 'exact size' and that prices include the 'war tax." Also note that the value of the jewelry illustrated has increased by as much as 5,000 (five thousand) per cent.

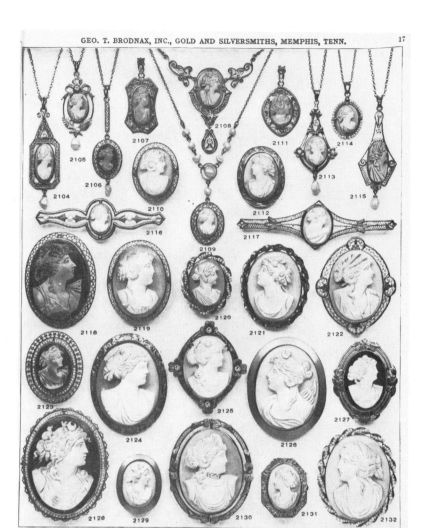

FINE 10 AND 14 KARAT CAMEO JEWELRY. (Illustrations exact size)

2104	Pink Cameo LaValliere, 1 diamond, 15-inch chain	$16.50
2105	Pink Cameo LaValliere, 1 diamond, green gold bow knot and leaves, 15-inch chain	
2106	Carnelian Cameo LaValliere, lacework mounting, 15-inch chain	11.50
2107	Coral Cameo Pendant, green gold, filigree mounting	6.00
2108	Pink Cameo Festoon, 4 diamonds in white gold settings, lacework mounting	11.50
2109	Pink Cameo Festoon, Baroque pearls, lacework mounting	26.50
2110	Pink Cameo Brooch, lacework mounting	12.50
2111	Coral Cameo Pendant, green gold, lacework mounting	6.50
2112	Pink Cameo Brooch, engraved mounting	10.00
2113	Pink Cameo LaValliere, 1 diamond and Baroque pearls, 15-inch chain	5.00
2114	Pink Cameo LaValliere, seed pearls, 15-inch chain	15.00
2115	14 kt. Coral Cameo LaValliere, 1 diamond, lacework mounting	6.00
2116	Pink Cameo Bar Pin, 4 Baroque pearls	20.00
2117	Pink Cameo Bar Pin, green gold, lacework mounting	7.50

*2118	Carnelian Cameo Brooch, lacework mounting	$15.00
†2119	Pink Cameo Brooch, lacework mounting	10.00
†2120	Pink Cameo Brooch, wreath of seed pearls	7.50
*2121	Pink Cameo Brooch, rope border	10.00
*2122	Pink Cameo Brooch, seed pearls, lacework mounting	14.50
†2123	Carnelian Cameo Brooch, seed pearls	10.00
2124	Pink Cameo Brooch, hand engraved mounting	11.00
2125	Pink Cameo Brooch, 4 diamonds in green gold leaves	35.00
2126	Pink Cameo Brooch, plain mounting, English	10.00
*2127	Sardonica Cameo Brooch, hand engraved mounting	10.00
*2128	Sardonica Cameo Brooch, seed pearls	23.50
†2129	Pink Cameo Brooch, plain polished mounting	5.00
†2130	Pink Cameo Brooch, white gold beeband with 3 diamonds, lacework mounting	30.00
2131	Pink Cameo Brooch, hand engraved mounting, octagonal shape	6.00
*2132	Pink Cameo Brooch, wreath of seed pearls	15.00

†These brooches are fitted with safety catches. *These brooches are fitted with safety catches and pendant rings.
These prices include war tax. We prepay all forwarding charges and guarantee safe delivery.

PLATE # - C - 4A

COMMENTS- Excerpt from a 1919 catalog. Note that the illustrations are 'exact size' and that prices include the 'war tax.' Also note that the value of the jewelry illustrated has increased by as much as 5,000 (five thousand) per cent.

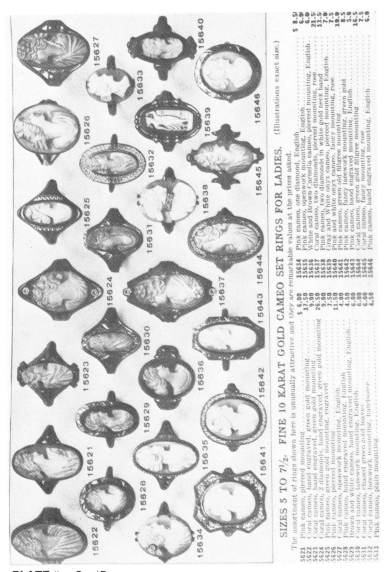

SIZES 5 TO 7½. FINE 10 KARAT GOLD CAMEO SET RINGS FOR LADIES. (Illustrations exact size.)

The assortment of rings shown here is unusually attractive and they are remarkable values at the prices asked.

No.	Description	Price
5621	Pink cameo, pierced mounting	$6.00
5622	Coral cameo, hand engraved, green gold mounting	17.50
5623	Coral cameo, hand engraved, green gold mounting	9.00
5624	Coral cameo, 2 diamonds, hand engraved, green gold mounting	26.50
5625	Pink cameo, green gold mounting	7.50
5626	Pink cameo, pierced mounting	11.50
5627	Coral cameo, openwork mounting, English	4.00
5628	Pink cameo, hand engraved mounting, English	4.50
5629	Flower and white cameo, hand engraved mounting, English	6.00
5630	Coral cameo, lacework mounting, English	6.00
5631	Coral cameo, chased green gold leaves	6.00
5632	Coral cameo, lacework mounting, handsome	7.50
5633	Pink cameo, plain mounting	

No.	Description	Price
15634	Pink cameo, one diamond, English	$8.50
15635	Pink cameo, openwork mounting, English	6.00
15636	White and Brown Cornelia cameo, pierced mounting, English	6.00
15637	Coral cameo, two diamonds, pierced mounting, rose	21.50
15638	Coral cameo, two diamonds in white gold neck band	13.50
15639	Gray and White onyx cameo, fancy mounting, English	7.00
15640	Pink and white onyx cameo, fancy mounting, rose	7.50
15641	Pink cameo, green old filigree mounting	18.00
15642	Pink cameo, fancy lacework mounting, green gold	8.50
15643	Pink cameo, fancy engraved mounting, English	5.00
15644	Coral cameo, green gold filigree mounting	16.50
15645	Coral cameo, fancy mounting, rose	7.50
15646	Pink cameo, hand engraved mounting, English	6.00

PLATE # - C - 4B
COMMENTS- Excerpt from a 1919 catalog. Note that the illustrations are 'exact size' and that the prices include the 'war tax.' Also note that the value of the jewelry illustrated has increased by as much as 5,000 (five thousand) per cent.

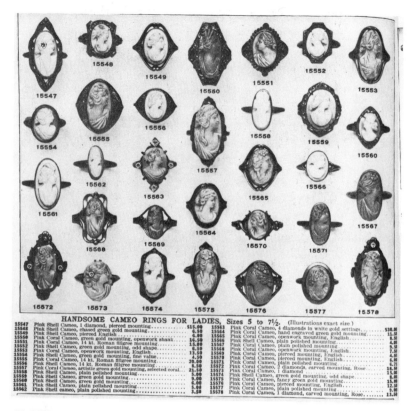

HANDSOME CAMEO RINGS FOR LADIES, Sizes 5 to 7½. (Illustrations exact size.)

No.	Description	Price		No.	Description	Price
15547	Pink Shell Cameo, 1 diamond, pierced mounting	$15.00		15563	Pink Coral Cameo, 4 diamonds in white gold settings	$38.00
15548	Pink Shell Cameo, chased green gold mounting	6.50		15564	Pink Coral Cameo, hand engraved green gold mounting	11.50
15549	Pink Shell Cameo, pierced English	6.90		15565	Pink Coral Cameo, openwork mounting, English	8.50
15550	Pink Coral Cameo, green gold mounting, openwork shank	16.50		15566	Pink Shell Cameo, plain polished mounting	4.00
15551	Pink Coral Cameo, 14 kt. Roman filigree mounting	15.00		15567	Pink Coral Cameo, plain polished mounting	9.50
15552	Pink Shell Cameo, green gold mounting, odd shape	6.50		15568	Pink Coral Cameo, openwork mounting, English	7.50
15553	Pink Coral Cameo, openwork mounting, English	13.50		15569	Pink Coral Cameo, pierced mounting, English	4.50
15554	Pink Shell Cameo, green gold mounting, fine value	4.50		15570	Pink Coral Cameo, pierced mounting, English	6.00
15555	Pink Coral Cameo, 14 kt. Roman filigree mounting	20.00		15571	Pink Coral Cameo, plain polished mounting	6.75
15556	Pink Shell Cameo, 14 kt. Roman filigree mounting	8.50		15572	Pink Coral Cameo, 2 diamonds, carved mounting, Rose	16.50
15557	Pink Coral Cameo, artistic green gold mounting, selected coral	21.50		15573	Pink Coral Cameo, 1 diamond	15.00
15558	Pink Shell Cameo, plain polished mounting	5.90		15574	Pink Shell Cameo, green gold mounting, odd shape	8.00
15559	Pink Shell Cameo, green gold mounting	9.00		15575	Pink Coral Cameo, fancy green gold mounting	15.00
15560	Pink Shell Cameo, green gold mounting	6.00		15576	Pink Coral Cameo, pierced mounting, English	12.50
15561	Pink Shell Cameo, plain polished mounting	5.90		15577	Pink Coral Cameo, plain polished mounting	9.00
15562	Pink Shell cameo, plain polished mounting	3.50		15578	Pink Coral Cameo, 1 diamond, carved mounting, Rose	13.50

PLATE # - C - 4C

COMMENTS- Excerpt from a 1919 catalog. Note that the illustrations are 'exact size' and that the prices include the 'war tax.' Also note that the value of the jewelry illustrated has incresed by as much as 5,000 (five thousand) per cent.

COMMENTS - All of the antique catalogue pages illustrated are from the collection of John Souizral of VBS, Endicott, N.Y. The catalogues are not for sale at the present time.

**GENNARO
BORRIELLO**

Gennaro Borriello s.r.l.   Branch in U.S.A.:
Via Montedoro, 1   12, Barberry Road
P.O. Box 145   West Islip
80059 Torre del Greco   New York 11795
(Napoli)   Tel. 1-800422.1631
Tel. 01139/81/8819835
Fax 01139/81/8491633
Telex 722522 GEBORR I

25

PLATE # - C - 5

YEAR - 1990

COMMENTS - Note that the actual sizes of the cameos shown are about double the photo size. This and the following photos are from the catalogues of five manufacturers of cameos, all based in Torre Del Greco in Italy. All had displays at the February, 1990 Jewelers of America show in New York City. Most of the cameos pictured are shell* cameos and are set in 14K gold, and most are available for $100 - $1,000. The cameos cannot be purchased from the manufacturers directly unless you visit their outlet shops in Torre del Greco, Italy in person. They can be purchased through the mail from **Artifacts - Box 455 - South View Station - Binghamton, New York 13903-0455** Write (or call 607-722-5619) for current prices. Also, your local jewelry store probably carries some cameos. Remember that no two shell cameos are exactly alike, since they are cut, carved, and set by hand. Each, is, in essence a customized piece of jewelry.
*Cornelian Helmet

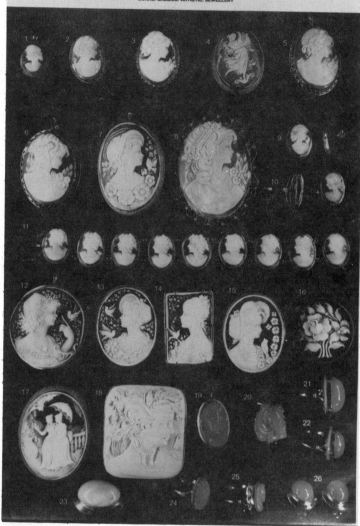

PLATE # - C - 5A

YEAR - 1990

COMMENTS - The cameos pictured in the lower right corner are coral cameos. Scenic cameos, such as no. 17, are usually carved from the more costly, darker background 'Sardonyx' Helmet shell and signed.

164

Iacobelli F.lli s.n.c.
Via Misericordia, 20
80059 Torre del Greco
(Napoli)
Tel. 01139/81/8491349
Fax 01139/81/8491637

63

PLATE # - C - 6

COMMENTS - The two cameos in the lower left that portray mythological figures are made of lava stone, which comes in various shades of gray, brown, and black.

Roberta s.r.l.
Via E. De Nicola, 2
80059 Torre del Greco
(Napoli)
Tel. 01139/81/8491966
Fax 01139/81/8492484
Telex 720220 APA I

90

PLATE # - C - 7

COMMENTS - The two cameos in the upper right that appear to have a white 'haze' around the edge are laser-cut stone cameos with assorted color backgrounds.

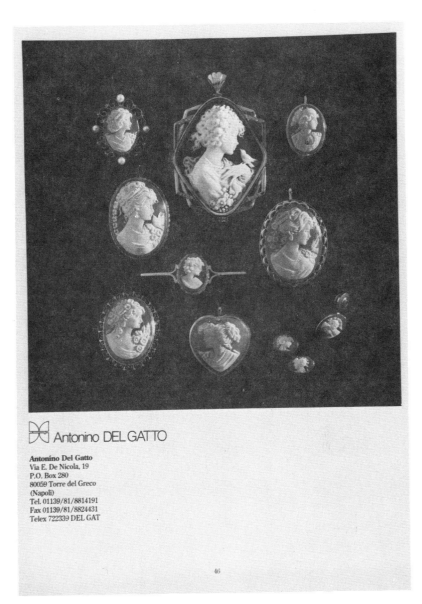

Antonino Del Gatto
Via E. De Nicola, 19
P.O. Box 280
80059 Torre del Greco
(Napoli)
Tel. 01139/81/8814191
Fax 01139/81/8824431
Telex 722339 DEL GAT

46

PLATE # - C - 8

COMMENTS - Pictured here are some quality carvings of women.

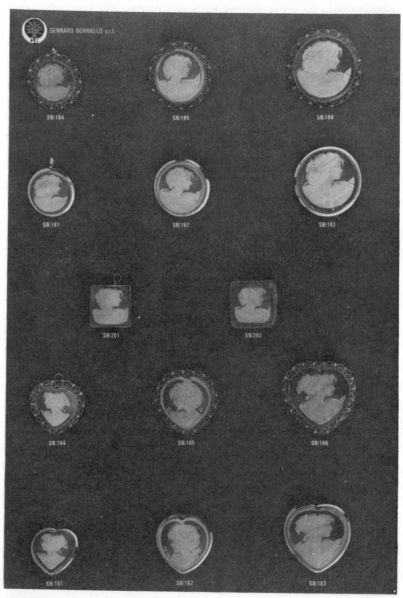

GENNARO BORRIELLO s.r.l.

SB/184 SB/185 SB/186

SB/181 SB/182 SB/183

SB/201 SB/202

SB/164 SB/165 SB/166

SB/161 SB/162 SB/163

PLATE # - C - 9

YEAR - 1990

COMMENTS - Cameos in assorted shapes.

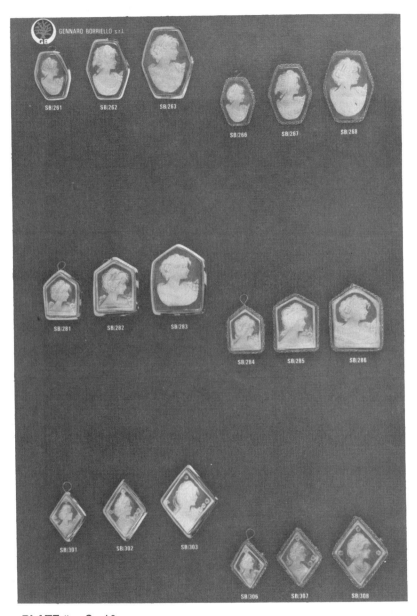

PLATE # - C - 10

YEAR - 1990

COMMENTS - Cameos in assorted shapes. These are available as combination pin/pendant.

169

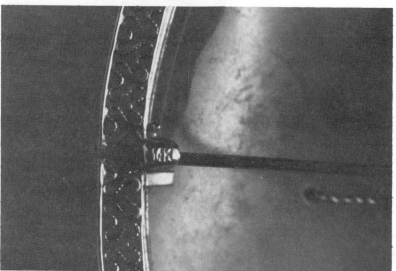

PLATE # - X - 1

COMMENTS - Detail of the backs of two cameos showing the "10k" and "14k" gold hallmarks.

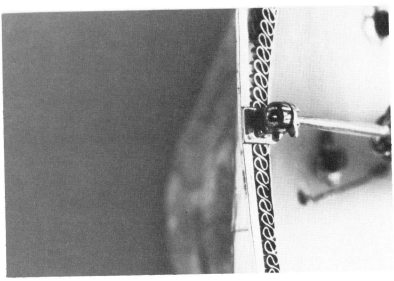

PLATE #- X - 2

COMMENTS - Detail of the backs of two cameos illustrating two different safety clasps for the pin.

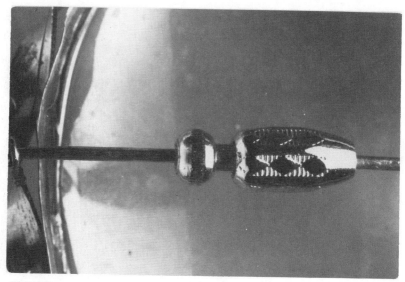

PLATE # - X - 2A

COMMENTS - Detail of a safety-slide that can be removed from the pin and is more often seen on stick pins.

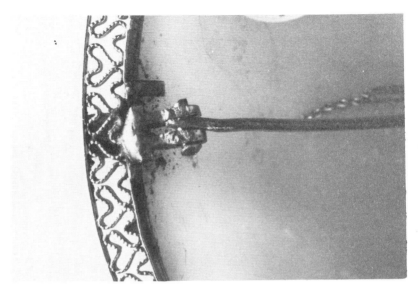

PLATE # - X - 3

COMMENTS - Detail of backside of a 1930's era cameo showing the pin-hinge.

PLATE # - X - 4

COMMENTS - Detail of the backs of two cameo frames showing two different hinge arrangements for the pin.

PLATE # - X - 5

COMMENTS - Detail of the backs of five different cameos illustrating various pendant-ring arrangements.

See following page

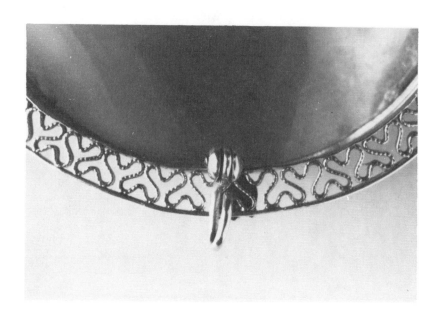

PLATE #X-6
Details of pendant ring arrangements.

PLATE #X-7
Details of pendant-ring arrangements.

BIBLIOGRAPHY

Abbott, R. Tucker, A Guide to Field Identification, Sea Shells of North America, New York, Golden Press, 1986.

Abbott, R. Tucker, Kingdom of the Seashell, New York, Crown Publishers, 1972.

Anderson, James, "Old-World Jewelry Made in America," Scientific American, Dec. 9, 1916.

"Art and Mythology in Cameos," Hobbies, November, 1947.

Avery, Charles, "A High Renaissance Cameo," The Connoisseur, Vol. 200, Jan., 1979.

"Bactria: Hub of the Great Trade Routes," National Geographic, March, 1990.

Ballard, Margaret, "Cameos -- From Art Form to Jewelry," Hobbies, August, 1975.

Bell, Jeanenne, Answers to Questions About Old Jewelry, 1840 to 1950, Alabama, Books of America, 1985.

Blumenthal, Deborah, "Cameos: Gift From the Sea," New York Times, August 5, 1989.

Bunt, Cyril G. E., "The Charm of the Cameo," Apollo, Vol. 74.

Burgess, Fred W., Antique Jewelry and Trinkets, New York, Tudor Pub., 1937.

"Cameo Cutting," Hobbies, May, 1951, reprinted from Chamber's Journal, April 5, 1884.

"Cameo Notes," Hobbies, September, 1948.

"Cameos and Their History," Scientific American, June 25, 1904.

Carr, Malcolm Stuart, "Tommaso and Luigi Saulini," The Connoisseur, Vol. 190, No., 1975.

Cavendish, Richard, Mythology, An Illustrated Encyclopedia, New York, Crescent Books, 1987.

Cocks, A. Somers, "Intaglios and Cameos in the Jewelery Collection of the V & A," Burlington, June 1976.

Cole, Gertrude S., "Cameos Cutters in America," Hobbies, July, 1947.

Cole Gertrude S., "Some American Cameo Portraitists."

Darlington, Ada, Antique Jewelry, Watkins Glen, N.Y., Century House, 1953.

Davenport, Cyril, Cameos, New York, The MacMillan Co., 1900.

Davenport, Cyril, "Cameos," Scientific American Supplement, No. 1315, March 16, 1901, No. 2107, Sept. 10, 1904.

Davenport, Cyril, "Cameos," The Smithsonian Report, 1904.

De Grummond, Nancy T., "The Real Gonzaga Cameo," American Journal of Archaeology, Vol. 78, 1974.

Dolan, Maryanne, "Portraits in Stone," Hobbies, July, 1982.

Evans, Joan, A History of Jewelry 1100-1870, New York, Dover Publications, 1970.

Fandel, Nancy, "The Cameo," Traditional Home, Oct., 1989.

Flower, Margaret, Victorian Jewelry, New York, Duell, Sloan & Pearce, 1951.

France, Alison, "Coreen Simpson, Cameo Designer," The New York Times, Feb. 25, 1990.

Goldemberg, Rose L., All About Jewelry, New York, Arbor House, 1983.

Goldemberg, Rose Leiman, Antique Jewelry. A Practical and Passionate Guide, New York, Crown Publishers, 1976.

Gonciar, Beth, "Her Majesty, The Cameo," Hobbies, February, 1948.

Bibliography cont'd.

"A Group of Shell Cameos," International Studio, November, 1925.

Hadley, Wayne, "Cameos," Rock and Gem, January, 1989.

Hamilton, Edith, Mythology, Boston, Little, Brown & Co., 1940.

Howard, Margaret Ann, "The Delicate Cameo," Lapidary Journal, November, 1988.

Jordan, Gladys, "Historic Cameos," Hobbies, June, 1952.

Lanllier, Jean and Pini, Marie-Anne, Five Centuries of Jewelry in the West, New York, Arch Cape Press, 1983.

Lessing, Eric, "The Cameo Carvers of Torre del Greco", Craft Horizons, 1951.

Masson, Georgina, "Two Thousand Years of Cameo Jewels," Apollo, March, 1976.

McCrory, Martha A., "Renaissance Shell Cameos from the Carrand Collection," Burlington, June, 1988.

Newman, Harold, An Illustrated Dictionary of Jewelry, New York, Thames & Hudson, Ltd., 1981.

"Notes on the History of Cameos," Hobbies, October, 1949.

Ritchie, C.I.A., Carving Shells and Cameos, Cranbury, N.J., A.S. Barnes & Co., 1970.

Ritchie, C.I.A., Shell Carving, History and Techniques, Cranbury, N.J., A.S. Barnes & Co., 1974.

Rogers, Julia E., The Shell Book, Boston, Charles T. Cranford Co., 1908.

Rosenberg, Pierre, "On the Origins of a Cameo at Versailles," Burlington, August, 1977.

Sasscier, Agnes L., "Cameo Cycle," Hobbies, April, 1941.

Scarisbrick, Diana, "Gem Connoisseurship," Burlington, Vol. 129 Feb., 1987.

Scherer, Barrymore L., "Cameo Appearances," Antiques, May, 1988.

Schumann, Walter, Gemstones of the World, New York, Sterling Publishing Co., 1977.

Seidmann, Gertrud, "Wilhelm Schmidt, the Last Neo-Classical Gem Engraver," Apollo, Vol. 128, July, 1988.

Sordillo, Art, "Jewelry With a Past," Traveler's Journal, 1988.

Tagliamonte, Nino, "History of Shell Cameos," Lapidary Journal, May, 1984.

Tait, Hugh, Jewelery Through 7,000 Years, London, British Museum Publications, Ltd., 1976.

Verrill, A. Hyatt, Shell Collector's Handbook, New York, G.P. Putnam's Sons, 1950.

Verril, A. Hyatt, Strange Sea Shells and Their Stories, Boston, L.C. Page & Co., 1936.

"The Milton Weil Collection of Cameos and Intaglios," Metropolitan Museum of Art Bulletin, April, 1940.

Zeitner, June Culp, "The Fine Art of Gem Engraving," Lapidary Journal, November, 1988.

ADDENDUM TO BIBLIOGRAPHY

Encyclopedia Britannica - Micropaedia Vol. II, 1974, U.S.A.

Feild, Rachael, Victoriana, Macdonald & Co., 1988.

The Jewels of Italy, Italian Institute For Foreign Trade, Rome, Italy.

Schrire, T. Hebrew Magic Amulets, Behrman House, N.Y., N.Y., 1982.

Tagiomonte, Nino and Lorraine, "Vitreous Paste Gem Carving", Lapidary Journal, March, 1990.

Webster's New Universal Unabridged Dictionary, Simon & Schuster, N.Y., N.Y., 1983.

World Book Encyclopedia (and Dictionary), Field Enterprises, U.S.A., 1975.

ABOUT THE PHOTOGRAPHS

The majority of the photographs were shot by Mr. Aswad and are done in black and white in order to graphically illustrate the details of each cameo. Color can detract from particular details. Color and/or black and white photos, including enlargements, are available from the authors. Write for details. The camera used was a professional model MP-3 Copy Camera. A 4" x 5" fixture (light tent) was fabricated by the photographer to soften the light. One spotlight with a freznel lens was utilized to enhance the texture of the carvings. At times, a small reflector was also used to highlight the opposing side of the cameo frame. The cover photo was taken with a 4" x 5" Horseman View Camera utilizing a 210mm lens. The film used was Kodak Ektachrome Transparency.

Photo enlargements or copies can be ordered from the photographer. Write to:

Carriage House Photography
496 Chenango Street
Binghamton, New York 13901